Amendments, Change and the Stability of Constitutions

The numerous amendments to the Brazilian Constitution of 1988 have led many to question its effectiveness, stability, and legitimacy. These concerns resonate deeply with the Brazilian population and its political figures, some of whom advocate for drafting a new constitution. In this climate, this volume presents a timely and thorough quantitative and qualitative analysis of these amendments and the solidity of constitutions more generally. The book focuses on understanding the impact of these amendments on the Constitution's foundational framework. By examining the nature and extent of changes over three decades, the study directly addresses contemporary concerns about the evolving nature of Brazilian constitutional law. This analysis is particularly appropriate now, given the ongoing debates about the Constitution's adaptability and the potential need for a more stable or enduring framework. The insights gained contribute significantly to informed discussions on constitutional reform, the resilience of legal structures, and the management of constitutional change in a dynamic socio-political landscape. Employing methodology that can be applied to other countries, the book enhances the growing body of knowledge in the field of constitutional law regarding constitutional amendments and reform processes. The work will be a valuable resource for academics and researchers working in the areas of Constitutional Law and Politics, Legal Theory, and Comparative Law.

Guilherme Baena Fernandes de Godoy is a judicial law clerk at the Brazilian Superior Labor Court, Brasilia, Brazil.

Laila Maia Galvão is a Law Professor at the Brazilian Institute of Education, Development and Research (IDP), Brasilia, Brazil.

Rafael Silveira e Silva is a Law Professor at the Brazilian Institute of Education, Development and Research (IDP), Brasilia, Brazil.

Comparative Constitutional Change

Comparative Constitutional Change has developed into a distinct field of constitutional law. It encompasses the study of constitutions through the way they change and covers a wide scope of topics and methodologies. Books in this series include work on developments in the functions of the constitution, the organization of powers, and the protection of rights, as well as research that focuses on formal amendment rules and the relation between constituent and constituted power. The series includes comparative approaches along with books that focus on single jurisdictions, and brings together research monographs and edited collections which allow the expression of different schools of thought. While the focus is primarily on law, where relevant the series may also include political science, historical, philosophical, and empirical approaches that explore constitutional change.

Series editors:
Xenophon Contiades is Professor of Public Law, Panteion University, Athens, Greece and Managing Director, Centre for European Constitutional Law, Athens, Greece.
Thomas Fleiner is Emeritus Professor of Law at the University of Fribourg, Switzerland.
Alkmene Fotiadou is Research Associate at the Centre for European Constitutional Law, Athens, Greece.
Richard Albert is the William Stamps Farish Professor in Law and Professor of Government at the University of Texas at Austin, USA.

Also in the series:

Amendments, Change and the Stability of Constitutions
The Cathedral Constitution of Brazil
Guilherme Baena Fernandes de Godoy, Laila Maia Galvão and Rafael Silveira e Silva

For more information about this series, please visit: www.routledge.com/Comparative-Constitutional-Change/book-series/COMPCONST

Amendments, Change and the Stability of Constitutions

The Cathedral Constitution of Brazil

Guilherme Baena Fernandes de Godoy, Laila Maia Galvão, and Rafael Silveira e Silva

Routledge
Taylor & Francis Group
LONDON AND NEW YORK

First published 2027
by Routledge
4 Park Square, Milton Park, Abingdon, Oxon OX14 4RN

and by Routledge
605 Third Avenue, New York, NY 10158

Routledge is an imprint of the Taylor & Francis Group, an informa business

British Library Cataloguing-in-Publication Data
A catalogue record for this book is available from the British Library

Library of Congress Cataloging-in-Publication Data
Names: Godoy, Guilherme Baena Fernandes de author |
Galvão, Laila Maia author | Silva, Rafael Silveira e author
Title: Amendments, change and the stability of constitutions : the Cathedral
Constitution of Brazil / Guilherme Baena Fernandes de Godoy, Laila Maia Galvão,
and Rafael Silveira e Silva.
Description: Abingdon, Oxon [UK] ; New York, NY : Routledge, 2026. |
Series: Comparative constitutional change |
Includes bibliographical references and index. |
Identifiers: LCCN 2026016884 (print) | LCCN 2026016885 (ebook) |
ISBN 9781041153917 hardback | ISBN 9781041153924 paperback |
ISBN 9781003679202 ebook
Subjects: LCSH: Brazil. Constituição (1988) | Constitutional amendments–Brazil |
Constitutional law–Brazil | Constitutions–Brazil | LCGFT: Constitutions
Classification: LCC KHD29141988 .G63 2026 (print) | LCC KHD29141988 (ebook)
LC record available at https://lccn.loc.gov/2026016884
LC ebook record available at https://lccn.loc.gov/2026016885

ISBN: 978-1-041-15391-7 (hbk)
ISBN: 978-1-041-15392-4 (pbk)
ISBN: 978-1-003-67920-2 (ebk)

DOI: 10.4324/9781003679202

Typeset in Times New Roman
by Newgen Publishing UK

Access the Support Material: www.routledge.com/9781041153917

Contents

Introduction

It is often said that the Brazilian Constitution has been amended many times since its promulgation. While this is true in terms of the sheer number of amendments, the impact of these changes on the Constitution's core structure is not always considered. This distinction is crucial, as the seemingly excessive mutability of the Federal Constitution raises concerns about its effectiveness, stability, and even legitimacy—leading some political actors to advocate for a new constitution.

Therefore, it is important that the analysis of these amendments not focus solely on their quantity but also on the quality of the changes they introduce. After all, a constitution is meant to serve as the foundation of the state—a guiding framework. Amendments that do not alter this fundamental structure are less likely to affect the state's architecture or its functionality. After so many approved amendments, one must ask: has the essential structure of the Republic, inaugurated in 1988, been significantly altered?

The analysis undertaken in this work will not be limited to the organization of powers or the form of government. Instead, it will examine the entire constitutional text to identify elements that seem to demand constant attention from the legislature. Could this intense legislative activity reflect the Congress's attempt to address the evolving needs of Brazilian society?

A thorough investigation is required: Which articles have been amended the most? What topics have been recurrent in the amendments? Which amendments have resulted in minor or superficial changes, and which have brought about more significant transformations? Conversely, which parts of the text have remained stable over these thirty-plus years? These questions are essential

DOI: 10.4324/9781003679202-1

for understanding the true scope of the changes that the Brazilian Constitution has undergone.

However, prior to delving into the intricacies of the response, it is imperative to employ a comparative metaphor. The present study sets out to demonstrate that constitutionalism can be compared to the historical process of constructing historic buildings, such as European cathedrals, for example.

Cathedral constitutionalism

The construction of European cathedrals, when examined from both a historical perspective and an architectural analysis, reveals a process that transcended simple construction, incorporating spiritual, economic, and symbolic dimensions of the medieval period.

Cathedrals were the physical embodiment of divine power, representing the prestige and modernity of the communities that sponsored them. For medieval builders, constructing a cathedral was a symbolic emulation of the divine act of creation of the universe, carried out in stages that mirrored the Christian view of the world.

The duration of these works was considerable. The construction of the Notre Dame Cathedral in Paris commenced in 1163 and continued for 182 years until its completion in 1345. This uninterrupted period of building work is a testament to the commitment and dedication of the artisans and builders who toiled on the project. The construction of Cologne Cathedral, for instance, spanned six centuries, whereas Milan Cathedral, initiated in 1386, was not fully completed until 1965, a period of nearly six centuries. This extended timeline reflected the cyclical nature of the projects, with construction interrupted by wars, economic crises, and stylistic changes, allowing each generation to leave its architectural mark.

Consequently, such constructions frequently coincided with the transition from the ancient to the modern world. The architectural history of European cathedrals is characterized by two significant periods: the architectural style of the region is characterized by the influence of Romanesque and Gothic architecture. The latter was responsible for the most revolutionary structural solutions.

In the context of Romanesque architecture, spanning the period from the fifth to the eleventh century, builders confronted fundamental limitations that constrained vertical height. However, these limitations were also the foundation for the durability of these constructions. Gothic innovation, from the twelfth century onwards, revolutionized the construction logic through complementary technological elements that allowed for greater structural efficiency, material savings and aesthetic improvement.

Cathedrals have been recognized as monuments to a historical process that was integrated, wherein faith, technique, and social organization operated in harmony, sustained by the dedication of many generations. Nevertheless, repairs, technical and material developments continued to be pursued, thereby ensuring the symbolic and historical significance of these buildings was maintained.

In a manner analogous to the evolution of cathedrals, which necessitated the progressive overcoming of technical limitations and refinement over successive generations, the consolidation of a constitutional text proved to be an equally long and segmented process. The concept of normative architecture, therefore, does not emerge instantaneously from isolated political decisions; rather, it is constructed through a series of historical layers that demonstrate its pertinence, whilst simultaneously allowing for adjustments and innovations.

The basis of normative decisions is not totalizing rational choices, which would establish the complete structure of the text at once. Conversely, they are established through alterations, which may be marginal, and in succession to pre-existing structures, thereby combining continuity with innovation (Lindblom, 1959).

In order to provide a basis for comparison between the construction of cathedrals and the drafting and revision of constitutional texts, the following points are proposed: firstly, that the process is intergenerational; secondly, that progress occurs in stages that integrate technical and legal knowledge; thirdly, that significant innovations may arise not as a total replacement of previous structures, but as a technical improvement of their fundamental principles; and fourthly, that permanence rests less on immutability than on the capacity for continuous revision and updating.

The constitutional text is regarded as a legal edifice whose foundations were established by the first generation of constituents, yet whose final structure is dependent on the cumulative work of multiple generations, through constitutional interpretation, amendments, and editorial refinement.

The central argument of this study is that the processes involved in constitutional amendment and the regularity with which these occur should not be interpreted as a distortion or deviation from the original text. Instead, these processes should be regarded as a natural and progressive evolution. In a manner analogous to the enduring presence of cathedrals as living monuments that meld structural stability with perpetual adaptation, democratic constitutions attain a congruent synthesis: they establish foundational principles that withstand political erosion while enabling constant reinterpretation and normative enhancement.

Perennial or inconstant constitution: some evidence

Since its promulgation, the 1988 Constitution has been the target of numerous criticisms regarding the length of its text (Vieira & Barbosa, 2018) and, later, the perceived excess of amendments. Three decades after its enactment, it has accumulated more than a hundred amendments, with its text growing even longer (Arantes & Couto, 2019). However, the criticisms always seem to focus on the numerical dimension of the amendments, rather than on their content or practical effects.

For example, when it turned thirty in 2018, several debates were held about the number of times the Constitution had been amended, suggesting a fundamental flaw in its original drafting, or even a failure of purpose in the constitutional text (Vieira & Barbosa, 2018). However, without a detailed analysis of what has occurred in recent years, it is impossible to determine the real problem beyond the sheer number of amendments. If not all amendments carry the same weight (and they certainly do not), then seeking further data could reveal a different scenario.

The controversy over the frequent changes to the Constitution has been a recurring topic for years, whether in academia, electoral debates, or the press; there are always those advocating for a new constitution. However, it is necessary to delve deeper into the matter: how can one say that the Constitution has been overly amended without understanding the quality of these changes? Likewise, a new constitution will be of no use if the same supposed mistakes are repeated, meaning if the potential weaknesses of the current one are not identified. After all, a new constitution that is significantly shorter will not serve us if, over time, it too is filled with numerous additional articles.

As the cornerstone of any legal system, constitutions are meant to last a long time, possibly centuries. Still, a good founding constituent understands that such a work cannot remain frozen in time, and that adaptability is a necessary condition for its permanence (Maués, 2020, p. 2). This is evident in the world's leading constitutions, which are altered either through amendments or judicial interpretation (Lutz,

1994, p. 355). In Brazil, the phenomenon of constitutional amendment seems unique, as of 2025 there have already been 138 amendments, in addition to the six revision amendments. The Constitution, then, is not promulgated as a definitive text but is constructed over the years by various different legislatures, much like European cathedrals, whose construction took centuries and involved many generations, in a slow and continuous process of refinement and rebuilding.

However, Brazil is far from being the only case. The 1917 Mexican Constitution is considered the most amended in the world, with 737 reforms by 2020. In the Mexican context, this phenomenon stems from the interaction between the Judiciary and the Legislature, such that as the diversity and number of binding Supreme Court decisions increase, more amendments are passed. Thus, the actions of the highest judicial body in Mexico not only apply the constitution but also effectively revise it (Pozas-Loyo, Saavedra-Herrera & Pou-Giménez, 2022, p. 1). Therefore, just because a constitution is old does not necessarily mean it will have few amendments or that its text is stable enough for a low amendment rate.

The same is observed in the United States. Often, people have the impression that, since the US Constitution has only 27 amendments in 234 years, it has been altered very little, and that the American practice is to avoid changing the constitutional text. In reality, the difficulty of formal amendment imposed by Article V of that constitution is so great that other pathways had to be used to prevent society from drifting away from the fundamental law. As a result, many changes have been made outside the amendment process and without altering the text, through laws and judicial decisions (Strauss, 2000, pp. 1469–1473).

Another aspect in the US is that the Federal Constitution is so succinct that it resembles more an international treaty than the fundamental law of a country. While the American Constitution is laconic, the state constitutions follow the more common rule of being lengthier and frequently amended. As an example, using the notation (number of constitutions the state has had/age of the current constitution/number of amendments to the current constitution): Alabama (6/90/726), Arizona (1/79/109), California (2/112/471), Maryland (4/124/200), Massachusetts (1/211/116), New York (4/96/207), South Carolina (7/95/463), and Texas (5/115/326) (Lutz, 1994, p. 367).

The first issue that needs to be understood is why the Brazilian constitutional text is so large. The current Constitution resulted from a compromise between opposing political forces, with many corporatist and social interests embedded in the text to ensure constitutional protection, given the deep mistrust of future political forces (Vieira & Barbosa, 2018, pp. 135–136). This perception that the final text should contain as many guarantees as possible led to the largest constitution the country has ever had.

Take Article 5, for example. It provides for the fundamental rights and guarantees of citizens, with a total of seventy-eight clauses. The aim was to protect a broad range of rights, essentially a "super" bill of rights, reflecting the post-military regime atmosphere. The extended length of Article 5 represents the Constituent Assembly's sentiment of including as many protections as possible in the constitutional text, to avoid another episode of institutional rupture and violation of basic rights.

What happens with Article 5 is not an isolated phenomenon, however. Throughout the constitutional text, there are lengthy and detailed articles, due to the climate of political distrust. The same is true for the amendments to the Constitution.

The first amendment to the constitution occurred in 1992. Since then, the text has been amended every year—with the exception of 2018, due to the federal intervention in Rio de Janeiro. The apparent need for the National Congress to constantly return to the constituent process seems to be linked to the inclusion of public policies in the Constitution, beyond the traditional structuring of the State (Arantes & Couto, 2019). As public policies vary from one government to another, the Brazilian political charter would naturally need to be amended recurrently.

This amendment process has not only altered the original text but also resulted in a substantial increase in size. According to Arantes and Couto, the Constitution was 44% larger in 2018 than it was in 1988 (Arantes & Couto, 2019). In other words, national legislators seem to persist in their distrust of political forces and continue to entrench guarantees and objectives in the constitutional text, contradicting the notion that a smaller original constitution would not suffer from the same excess of amendments.

Indeed, it is worth noting that a smaller, principle-based text—as some advocate—would not necessarily lead to a better result. Ginsburg et al. point out the opposite: constitutions that are more detailed and encompass broader interests tend to last longer than shorter, more generalist ones (Elkins, Ginsburg & Melton, 2009, p. 8). In this sense, the Brazilian Constitution had broad popular participation in the first phase of its drafting (Vieira, 2018, pp. 135–149), something some consider essential when exercising original constituent power (Roznai, 2017, pp. 24–25).

Another peculiar characteristic of the derivative constituent process in Brazil is the judicialization of amendments. Although not frequent, the analysis of amendments by the Supreme Court is relatively expected after promulgation, as occurred with 35 amendments by 2018 (Oliveira & Arguelhes, 2021, p. 3). The vast majority of these refer to amendments considered public policy-related, reinforcing the argument that the Constitution's core has not been significantly altered.

While Arantes and Couto classify the amendments into polity (concerning state structures) and policy (concerning public policies), Maués separates them by the title altered in the Constitution. According to his division, the most amended title is Taxation and Budget, the subject of 41 amendments (Maués, 2020, p. 21). However, these classifications do not answer certain questions, such as: 1) which of the altered provisions have stabilized over time, i.e. have not been subject to further amendments after some changes; and 2) which amendments brought the least changes to the text structure, and which had the most impact. This is because a large number of amendments that change peripheral characteristics of the Constitution seem to reflect more a political inclination to appear as though changes are being made, rather than an actual desire to implement them, for example.

Therefore, the next chapters will delve deeper into the production of data, seek a more detailed historical analysis of the amendments, and find a definition of which parts of the constitutional text have become essential to the functioning of the country. It may seem paradoxical that one of the longest-standing constitutions of the republican period is constantly amended, but perhaps this is part of its strength—a sign that the social changes Brazil has undergone since redemocratization require renewed attention from time to time.

The initial part of this study provides a historical overview of Brazilian constitutionalism. This review outlines Brazil's constitutional evolution, highlighting the incorporation of new trends while maintaining certain political and legal designs. The first chapter, therefore, explores the concept of a "historical constitution" in Brazil by examining the institutional legacy passed down from one Constitution to another. Some provisions of the current Constitution have origins in previous ones, giving a sense that the Constitution is a long-term construction.

The second chapter outlines the methodology used for data collection and interpretation. To classify the impact of the amendments, the study introduces the "crystallization index" and "crystallization rate." These methodologies measure how amendments solidify existing law. By thoroughly analyzing all amendments to the 1988 Constitution and organizing them in various tables, the study draws conclusions about the most and least altered regions of the Constitution. This analysis allows us to examine this process over time and provides an accurate understanding of the real impact of these amendments on the constitutional text.

The third chapter presents a qualitative analysis of the amendments using the classification framework by Richard Albert. The amendments are categorized into corrective, elaborative, and dismemberment types. This categorization helps understand the nature of the changes made to the Constitution. The findings are compared with similar research to bolster the argument presented. The final part of this study integrates the historical, quantitative, and qualitative approaches to analyzing the Brazilian Constitution.

The conclusion states that the Constitution's essential core remains unchanged, indicating that certain sections are the primary focus of reform efforts. Most amendments served to refine or enhance the original framework. Only a few amendments have reversed elements of the Constitution as conceived in 1988. Nevertheless, it is suggested that removing certain articles from the Constitution could help reduce the need for frequent amendments.

Like centuries-old European cathedrals, which start small and are expanded, renovated, and improved over generations—a process measured in decades or even centuries—Brazilian constitutionalism has done the same. It has built new constitutions on the foundations of previous ones, creating what we can call our "Cathedral Constitution." Furthermore, readers are invited to refer to the appendices, which can be consulted on the book's website. These appendices serve as illustrative databases containing details that may be relevant for comparative studies and for verifying the information gathered in the research. They provide the empirical data, methodological documentation, and supporting materials underlying the analyses developed in this volume, with a particular focus on the amendment history and constitutional evolution of the Brazilian Constitution.

The following concise synopsis outlines the compendium of appendices made available for the benefit of the reader. Appendix A presents a table in which the amendments are ordered chronologically, listing all the articles that each amendment altered. In Appendix B there is a reverse table of the previous one, listing the articles in ascending order, along with all the amendments that affected them. Appendix C presents a table with the articles of the ADCT (Transitional Constitutional Provisions Act) in ascending order, with the corresponding amendments that reformed or created them. Appendix D shows the crystallization index and rate of each of the articles, and the years (1989 to 2025) in which they were modified. Appendix E presents a table in which the titles, chapters, and sections of the Constitution are ordered as they appear in the text, with each respective amendment listed, with a birds eye view of all modifications made. Appendix F presents a table in which the titles, chapters, and sections of the Constitution are ordered as they appear in the text, with the respective amendments listed chronologically, where each column represents a year (from 1989 to 2025), along with their crystallization index and rate. Appendix G shows an overview of the modifications to the Constitution, presenting the modified articles (and respective amendments) and unmodified articles. The table uses a "heat map" to visually highlight the most modified points of the Constitution and those that remain untouched. Finally, Appendix H presents a table in which the originating PECs (Proposed Constitutional Amendments) of the amendments are ordered chronologically and classified.

Appendix I shows a list of all classified amendments using Professor Richard Alberts' classification. In order to facilitate the smooth progression of the text, it has been deemed necessary to exclude the appendices from the main body of the publication. Nevertheless, as they constitute a valuable resource for reference and research, they have been made available to readers via the following link: www.routledge.com/9781003679202

References

Arantes, R. B., & Couto, C. (2019). 1988–2018: Trinta anos de constitucionalização permanente. In N. M. Filho & A. P. Souza (Eds.), *A carta: Para entender a Constituição brasileira*. São Paulo: Todavia.

de Oliveira, F. L., & Arguelhes, D. W. (2021). O Supremo Tribunal Federal e a mudança constitucional. *Revista Brasileira de Ciências Sociais*, 36(105), 1–20.

Elkins, Z., Ginsburg, T., & Melton, J. (2009). *The endurance of national constitutions*. Cambridge: Cambridge University Press.

Lindblom, C. E. (1959). The science of 'muddling through. *Public Administration Review*, 19(2), 79–88.

Lutz, D. S. (1994). Toward a theory of constitutional amendment. *American Political Science Review*, 88(2), 355–370.

Maués, A. M. (2020). 30 anos de constituição, 30 anos de reforma constitucional. *Revista Direito GV*, 16(1), 72–101.

Pozas-Loyo, A., Saavedra-Herrera, C., & Pou-Giménez, F. (2022). When more leads to more: Constitutional amendments and interpretation in Mexico, 1917–2020. *Law & Social Inquiry*, 50, 1–32.

Roznai, Y. (2017). Amendment power, constituent power, and popular sovereignty: Linking unamendability and amendment procedures. In Richard Albert, Xenophon Contiades, Alkmene Fotiadou (eds.). *The foundations and traditions of constitutional amendment* (pp. 23–49). Oxford and Portland, Oregon: Hart Publishing, an imprint of Bloomsbury Publishing Plc,

Strauss, D. A. (2000). The irrelevance of constitutional amendments. *Harvard Law Review*, 114, 1457–1505.

Vieira, O. V. (2018). A batalha dos poderes: Da transição democrática ao mal-estar constitucional. *Editora Companhia das Letras*.

Vieira, O. V., & Barbosa, A. L. P. (2018). Do compromisso maximizador à resiliência constitucional. *Novos Estudos Cebrap*, 37, 375–393.

1 The historical constitution

Amendment process in historical perspective

The power to amend constitutions has been the subject of scholarly attention since the first codified constitutions were enacted. In fact, the Constitution of the United States of America arose precisely in a context of revising the Articles of Confederation, which required unanimous approval from Congress in order to be amended (Ostrom & Allen, 2008, p. 7). This was one of the main innovations of the Articles of Confederation, which derived from the colonial tradition of conventions, understood as necessary to provide a mechanism for correcting any flaws identified in legal texts. What may seem trivial today actually originates from the American logic that constitutional documents should be subject to revision, a notion that did not exist before the Articles of Confederation (albeit in a primitive form) and the American Constitution itself (as it is known today). By way of example, Cromwell's Instruments of Government from 1653 did not include any provision for revision (Ostrom & Allen, 2008, p. 7).

The reason for allowing amendments to the constitutional text was based on the idea of popular sovereignty. In this conception, constitutional instruments were the product of the will of the people, who could rewrite them whenever they wished. Consequently, American state constitutions, like the Articles of Confederation, were to be drafted by a convention elected for that purpose, with the resulting document subsequently ratified by the people (Lutz, 1994). This same notion of popular power was expressed in France by Abbé Sieyès in his work *What is the Third Estate?*, written shortly before the French Revolution. In it, he argued for the existence of an unlimited and sovereign Constituent Power (*pouvoir constituant*), arising from the

DOI: 10.4324/9781003679202-2

popular will, and a Constituted Power (*pouvoirs constitués*), whose ability to act is limited by the constituent power. This power should be exercised by an assembly chosen by the people, in which extraordinary representatives act on behalf of the Nation (Klein, 1978, p. 210–211).

In addition to the principle of popular sovereignty, the power of amendment was based on three central principles of American thought from the 1770s: the imperfect but educable nature of humanity, the effectiveness of the deliberative process, and the distinction between ordinary legislation and constitutional matters (Lutz, 1994, p. 356).

The first principle is based on the idea of human fallibility; therefore, popular government should reflect this characteristic of human nature. It was understood that every governmental institution has an aspect of experimentation and that, as such, they could be improved when necessary, with the constitution containing mechanisms for the people to make such changes. The second principle is the need for a deliberative process so that collective decisions are made efficiently. From this principle comes the understanding that the more essential the matter to be considered, the greater the deliberation that should occur before such a decision. Lastly, the third principle states that constitutional matters are more important than ordinary legislation and, therefore, not only should the deliberative process for this type of legislation be more prolonged, but the approval process for constitutional amendments should also have a more complex regime (Lutz, 1994, p. 356–357).

The process of amending a constitution arises from and is justified by the need to make adjustments to the constitutional text so that it legitimately corresponds to the expectations of the population. A constitution is nothing more than a contract—as proponents of the contractualist theory used to say (Laskar, 2013)—between the members of a given national community, aimed at organizing the exercise of power, limiting it, and guiding how it should act to achieve the objectives set forth in the fundamental law. Thus, the constitution is, at once, the beginning (or foundation) of the legal order and also its endpoint (or ceiling), from where laws originate and at the same time the limit they cannot surpass.

However, the issue of the power to amend constitutions is not as simple as the power to alter ordinary laws. This is because the authority that enacts ordinary legislation is the same authority that may amend or repeal it, as authorized by the constitution. By contrast, the power that enacts the constitution is not the same as the power that carries out constitutional amendments, a distinction that entails important practical implications. Analogously, it would be as if the authority that issues an ordinance tried to modify a law. This is not possible because they do not possess the same power, and there is a clear hierarchy between them. This phenomenon did not go unnoticed at the first US Congress when, during a debate about the ten amendments that would become known as the Bill of Rights, there was a question as to whether they would become part of the constitution's main body or, conversely, if they would only be appended at the end of the text, not actually incorporated into the document (Klein, 1978, p. 210). While the Secretary of State, James Madison, argued that the amendments should be blended into the original constitution's text, Representative Sherman believed that they would form part of the constitutional order but not the text of the constitution itself: In other words, how could the power to amend the constitution modify the very foundation that supports it? Sherman's position prevailed, so amendments are appended at the end of the original text, but the understanding that took hold in the United States is that they belong to the body of the constitution (Klein, 1978, p. 210).

This debate may seem strange today, but it is quite enlightening regarding how the concepts of amendment power were not yet well defined at the beginning of American constitutionalism, and how amendment theories were still undeveloped. Even the notion of unconstitutional amendments is not settled in American doctrine, as there are no explicit amendment limitations (that is, entrenched clauses)[1]. Some, however, believe there are implicit limitations that prevent an amendment from disfiguring the constitutional system and its purposes, while others believe the amendment power is unlimited (Roznai, 2013, p. 670–672).

It is equally important to understand the use of the term "amendment," used in the US Constitution, and what the founders' intent was in choosing this word. In the case of Rhode Island v. Palmer, it was argued that the founders' intention in using the term "amendment" was the same as that established in common law; that

1 The limitations were: not abolishing the slave trade or altering rules on direct taxes before 1808 (Art. V in conjunction with Art. I, section 9, clauses 1 and 4). It is also not possible to reduce a state's representation in the Senate without its consent (Art. V in conjunction with Art. 1, section 3, clause 1), with the latter still in effect today.

is, to amend means only to correct errors in the constitution, not to introduce substantive changes to the original text that could subvert the Founding Fathers' intent. This argument was not accepted by the US Supreme Court (Roznai, 2013, p. 670–672). However, this understanding was incorporated in other countries, such as France and Germany.

As previously mentioned, Sieyès was the one who introduced in France the notion of constituent power and constituted power, distinguishing them by the holder who exercises the power. While only the "people" (through special representatives) could form a new constitution, the national assembly would be authorized only to amend the text written by the sovereign, and therefore this power would be limited by nature. This distinction led to the emergence of the French theory of "original constituent power" and "derived constituent power," which spread across continental Europe and is also used in Brazil. Even though there was no notion of entrenched clauses, it was understood that it was not possible to change the form of government (frame of government) established by the people. In Germany, authors such as Carl Schmitt also distinguished between the power to create a constitution and the power to amend it (Klein, 1978, p. 212).

The end of the so-called Liberal State of the 19th century and the emergence of the Social State at the beginning of the 20th century weakened the separation between original and derived constituent power, while the notion of parliamentary supremacy gained strength, eventually becoming mainstream thought in Europe, especially in France and Germany in the 1920s and 1930s. During this period, successive worldwide economic crises—particularly after the 1929 Crisis—increasingly pressured the Social State, which, to meet growing popular demands, ended up allocating even greater powers to the Executive. This extreme delegation of legislative powers to the Executive represented an abandonment process of the 19th-century constitutional ideals of separation of powers (Lindseth, 2004, p. 1347–1348).

Thus, it is possible to observe that original constituent power became intertwined with the legislature itself, even though the legislature is a constituted structure. This is because the unrestricted delegation of powers to the Executive clearly violates the notion of separation of powers, in an apparent perception that parliament, speaking on behalf of the people, would be democratically legitimizing this transfer of competencies. It was perhaps an excess of democracy that ended up undermining itself, demonstrating—at least initially—the need to distinguish the power to legislate from constituent power.

After the war, discussions arose on how to prevent a new degeneration into authoritarianism in Germany. The architects of the 1949 Basic Law defined a set of fundamental rights, as well as the main responsibilities of the Legislature that could not be delegated under any circumstances. They also established an external body to parliament with the power to stop the Legislature in case of breach of these constitutional rules, the Federal Constitutional Court (Lindseth, 2004, p. 1349). Article 79, paragraph 3 of the Basic Law introduced the provision that articles 1 to 20 are entrenched clauses, inalienable even by parliamentary amendment power, thus ending parliamentary supremacy and inaugurating constitutional supremacy.

It can be seen so far that the nature of the amendment power originated from a debate about how constituent power should be exercised, and whether there should be symmetry between the way a constitution is written and the way it is amended. While one school believes amendment power serves only as a means to correct course—prohibiting substantial changes to the original text (frame of government)—another school maintains that there are no limitations on changing the constitution, and the Legislature is free to make whatever changes it deems necessary. To prevent the constitution from being gradually and completely altered, and even subverted in its original meaning, some countries have adopted the idea of entrenched clauses, making it clear that derived constituent power does not have the authority for substantial changes and is therefore indeed limited and exercised as a delegation of original constituent power.

The nature of amendments must be well defined, as the analysis of what constitutes such change, especially in countries that adopt judicial review, is entirely dependent on the meaning given to the scope of amendment power. Could a parliament write a new constitution solely through amendments? If this is possible, then there seems to be no constitutional supremacy, but rather a code of laws with constitutional form. It seems unreasonable for it to be so. As previously stated, the constitution is the very origin of the legal system, its beginning, and the Legislature is its creation, with clear boundaries as to how its power should be exercised. Constituent power, by contrast, knows no limits or formulas. It is a power exercised not based on Law (because it creates the Law), but on philosophical and social grounds.

Amendment power, on the other hand, lies on the border of Law, but still within it.

Perhaps because these distinctions were still very recent, the Founding Fathers chose four formulas for amending the US Constitution. They are (article V of the US Constitution): (i) Congress proposes a constitutional change by a two-thirds quorum, and the proposal becomes valid when ratified by at least three-quarters of the states, through their respective legislatures; (ii) Congress proposes a constitutional change by a two-thirds quorum, and the proposal becomes valid when ratified by state conventions in at least three-quarters of the states; (iii) Two-thirds of the states send a petition to Congress for it to convene a constitutional convention to propose a constitutional change, and the proposal of the convention becomes valid when ratified by at least three-quarters of the states, through their respective legislatures; or (iv) Two-thirds of the states send a petition to Congress for it to convene a constitutional convention to propose a constitutional change, and the proposal becomes valid when ratified by state conventions in at least three-quarters of the states.

This complex process is at the root of why there have been only 27 amendments to the US Constitution. It is important to note that one of the amendment methods in the American Constitution is very similar to the one used to create the Constitution itself. The 1787 Philadelphia Convention used, for the new constitution's entry into effect, the formula of ratification by state conventions in at least nine states (Article VII). This method is exactly the same as the last formula on the list above, with one exception: ratification required nine states, one less than the three-quarters rule in Article V, which—given the number of states at the time—would be ten states (three-quarters of thirteen states).

The nature of amendment power was at the heart of the discussions about ratifying the American Constitution, and it explains why there are these four forms of amendment. The Federalists believed that a stronger national government was necessary, one that could better address the country's problems legislatively and executively, especially regarding credits and contracts (Holton, 2008). However, Article 13 of the Articles of Confederation stipulated that any amendment to that constitution had to be approved unanimously by the state legislatures. To propose a new constitution, the Federalists would have to submit the new text for approval by the assemblies, and they knew they would not have the necessary support, since the new text provided for a reduction in the power of the states (Ackerman & Katyal, 1995, pp. 478–480, 516, 546, 562).

Initially, the Federalists requested that a convention be called in Philadelphia to discuss amendments to the Articles of Confederation, which was approved by the Continental Congress. The congressional resolution expressly stated that the Convention should review the Articles of Confederation, send suggestions to Congress, and then to the state legislatures for ratification, so that the federal constitution (in this case, the Articles of Confederation) would meet the needs of the government and the Union. However, this was not done by the Convention, and this point is important for our analysis.

Article 7 of the new proposed constitution stated that it would take effect once ratified by state conventions (not legislatures), and without Congress analyzing the text. This not only diverged from the approved congressional resolution but was clearly illegal, and therefore unconstitutional. So, how could a new regime be approved in such blatant violation of the existing rules? Ackerman demonstrates that the Founders did not resort to legalistic arguments to defend the new constitutional text, but used revolutionary rhetoric to justify that the "people," when they so wished, could abandon a regime they deemed inferior and adopt a better one, just as they did when severing ties with the United Kingdom (Ackerman & Katyal, 1995, pp. 478, 488–489, 506–507, 530–531, 562).

To justify that the method of adopting the new constitution was not illegal but legitimate, they argued that state conventions should ratify or not the new text—and not the state legislatures, which were subject to the state constitutions—since power belonged to the people (thus aligned with the American doctrine of popular sovereignty). This strategy had historical precedents. The use of the "convention" institution not only to bring a new constitution to the old order, but also to make amendments to the new constitution, has historical origins. In the past, when it was not possible to hold a parliamentary session, the English used a convention to allow a parallel legislature to function. Thus, the Federalists did the same, and to break the old order without the need for a revolution, the Founders resorted to the "convention" mechanism as a bridge to the new constitutional regime (Ackerman & Katyal, 1995, pp. 559–561):

> This great precedent provided the Federalists with a language that permitted them to present their rule-breaking initiative in a way

> that allowed them to fall short of total revolution. As in the English case, the Federalist break with the legal rules did not mark an utter and complete repudiation of the institutional past. The Federalist conventions of 1787–88, like the English Convention a century earlier, had made a credible effort to link their pedigree with institutional elements of the preexisting constitution.
>
> (Ackerman & Katyal, 1995, p. 560)

In this way, the Founders did not completely break with the constitutional environment, or rather, with the constitutional culture. It was a revolution, but a controlled revolution. As they transitioned from one regime to another, there was continuity, with careful attention to keeping the old Congress functioning until the transition was complete—after the election of the new Congress—already under the new constitutional order (Ackerman & Katyal, 1995, pp. 515, 521–522, 556–557). Presumably, to prevent a single state or state elites from blocking any future and necessary constitutional reform (even if that meant a new constitution), the new Charter provided for four methods of amendment, including one identical to the formula used to ratify the US Constitution. This could suggest that the Founders did not strictly distinguish between the power of amendment and the power of founding, since both powers exist in the amendment article of the constitution (Article 5). This is the theory espoused by Professor Richard Albert.

Albert differentiates amendments from what he calls constitutional dismemberment. An amendment, according to him, can be elaborative or corrective; the latter should be used to improve the text at its foundations, promoting corrections for this purpose. An elaborative amendment brings about a change greater than a simple correction, continuing the process of constitution-making and expanding its original intentions, while dismemberment brings about a more radical reform:

> A constitutional dismemberment alters a fundamental right, a load-bearing structure, or a core feature of the identity of a constitution. It is a constitutional change understood by political actors and the people to be inconsistent with the constitution at the time the change is made. To use a rough shorthand, the purpose and effect of a constitutional dismemberment are the same: to unmake a constitution.
>
> (Albert, 2018, p. 4)

In this sense, a change made by an amendment (or amendments), even if the same constitution remains, will be a dismemberment when it reorients a constitutional subsystem, contrary to what the framers intended. According to Albert, this is not necessarily good or bad; it depends on what is being changed. The example the author uses is the Reconstruction amendments after the American Civil War. Amendments 13, 14, and 15 removed the slave system in the constitution, clearly opposing what the founders wanted—particularly since they had expressly prohibited any amendment to abolish the slave trade in the US before the year 1808. With these reforms, the text established that there could be no racial discrimination and abolished the three-fifths clause, the fugitive slave clause, and proportional taxation. The dismemberment was clearly positive, and kept the same constitution, now reoriented.

Professor Albert's theory is one that will be used in this research to better understand the phenomenon of amendment in Brazil, and how this constituent power has been exercised in the country. By classifying amendments in a way that considers the effect they have on the constitutional text, the theory can be a valuable tool in showing that not all amendments are equal in Brazil, and distinguishing them may demonstrate how preserved the 1988 Constitution is.

From all that has been discussed so far, it is possible to understand that the nature and power of amendment are not as trivial as they may sometimes appear, especially when, in Brazil, this same power is so much used that it becomes mundane (and arguably even banal). On the contrary, the amendment power carries a series of historical issues that are fundamental to understanding its exercise. Far from being a simple legislative process, it is actually quite peculiar, as it can even alter the original meaning of a constitution, as theorized by Professor Albert. As the first practice of the modern constitutional system, studying the US mechanism is essential to understanding the roots of amendment power and how it relates to original constituent power. As a living fossil, the US Constitution and its legislative practices help us understand the reasons that led the founders to adopt such a system for altering the constitutional text.

Amendment process in Brazilian constitutions

The power of amendment in Brazil has essentially been exercised the same way since the proclamation of the Republic. Unlike the United

States, Brazil did not experience a major debate over the extent of amendment power. By the time the 1891 Constitution was adopted, the American amendment process was already well established, with over a hundred years of experience (Nogueira, 2012, p. 12–13).

On the other hand, the 1824 Brazilian Constitution, the longest-lasting in Brazil, was exceptional not only for its longevity, but also for its amendment practice, or rather, for the near absence of amendments during the imperial regime. Officially, the 1824 Constitution had only one amendment, the so-called Additional Act of 1834, which introduced a few changes to the text. However, the constitutional regime of the Empire was, in practice, substantially altered over its 65 years of existence.

Octaciano Nogueira notes that the immense plasticity of the Imperial Constitution was one of the main elements responsible for its durability (Nogueira, 2012, p. 11), especially because it did not contain any entrenched clause that would limit the derived constituent power, as the Brazilian 1824 Constitution stated in its article number 178: "Only what concerns the limits and respective attributions of the Political Powers, and the Political and individual Rights of Citizens, is Constitutional. Everything that is not Constitutional can be changed without the aforementioned formalities, by ordinary Legislatures." Nogueira himself comments that the Republic could have been implemented with the 1824 Constitution, requiring only an amendment for that purpose (Nogueira, 2012, p. 11).

The aforementioned formalities refer to the legislative process for amending the constitution, which was unique in our political history, as observed from article 173 to article 177 of the 1824 Constitution. In summary, the main issues regarding this amendment process were: (i) Except for the first four years of the 1824 Constitution, in any legislature, a proposal to amend the constitution could be presented in the Chamber of Deputies, subscribed to by at least one-third of them; (ii) The proposal would be read once every six days, at which point it could be discussed and voted on, just like any other bill; (iii) The approved ordinary law would be sanctioned by the Emperor, stating in its text that voters, when choosing candidates in the next election, would also be authorizing the constitutional change provided for in the same law, i.e., it already contained the articles of the constitution that could be modified in the future; (iv) In the first session of the following legislature, the matter would be discussed and voted on in ordinary procedure, and a law would be approved declaring which changes were made to the constitution.

The only amendment to the Imperial Constitution that followed this procedure was the Law 16 (enacted in August 12, 1834), which became known as the Additional Act of 1834. It promoted a series of reforms. It should be noted that the constitutional practice of the time did not actually change what was written in the constitution. It merely added the new Act, somewhat similar to what happened in the US, where approved amendments were appended to the end of the constitution without mixing them into the original text. This system also greatly limited Parliament's amendment power, as deputies could only change what was in a specific law, not being able to revise articles outside of it.

Despite being the only formally approved amendment of the period, Nogueira states that the Empire's constitutional system was substantially altered during its six decades of existence, since the constitution was strongly complemented by ordinary legislation. Likewise, political practice led the Empire towards a parliamentary regime, even though there was no such provision in the Empire's Constitution (Nogueira, 2012, p. 13). The plasticity of the 1824 Charter was in full operation.

The absence of a political regime in the Imperial Constitution allowed the country to mature into a *de facto*, if not *de jure*, parliamentary system. By law, direct voting was instituted (the so-called Saraiva Law) and slavery was abolished, without the need to amend the constitution (an important difference from the US, considering that the US constitutionalized the slave system in different articles). These were important legislative and political changes, without altering the constitution. When it was repealed in 1889, it was the second oldest written constitution in the world, after that of the US (Nogueira, 2012, p. 10).

The 1891 Constitution of the Republic, although not lasting as long as the imperial one, endured a long (by Brazilian standards) 40 years, having also been amended only once. The amendment process of the 1891 Constitution, described in article 90, inaugurated the method that would be adopted, with minor modifications, throughout the entire republican life of the country. In summary, the amendment proposal should be either presented by at least one quarter of the deputies; or at least one quarter of the senators; and approved in three rounds of discussion and voting, by at least two-thirds, in both Houses, as follows: (i) first discussion and vote by two-thirds in the Chamber of Deputies; (ii) second discussion and vote by two-thirds in the

Chamber of Deputies; (iii) third discussion and vote by two-thirds in the Chamber of Deputies; (iv) first discussion and vote by two-thirds in the Senate; (v) second discussion and vote by two-thirds in the Senate; and (vi) third discussion and vote by two-thirds in the Senate. Or the amendment should be requested by two-thirds of the states, each expressing itself by the simple majority of their respective assemblies, within one year from the first state manifestation.

Once approved by either of the two methods above, it would be submitted to the Congress Houses in the following year, using the same method of discussion and approval as referred to above (first discussion and vote by two-thirds in the Chamber of Deputies, second discussion and vote, etc.).

It is clear that the system described above created the basis for what is still used today: multi-round discussion by qualified quorum (at the time, two-thirds), but with an important detail, the one-year interstice. This is perhaps one reason why the 1891 Constitution was amended only one time, as it was much slower to amend the constitutional text. Another aspect of the new amendment regime is the express provision that the reformed text would be integrated (incorporated) into the constitution, leaving behind the system of appending (from the imperial Brazilian Constitution of 1824 and the US Constitution) and adopting the integrative system (Cunha, 2023, p. 77).

Finally, for the first time, the institution of entrenched clauses was used, in § 4 of article 90, prohibiting reforms that alter the Republic, the Federation, and the equality of representation in the Senate (this last one clearly inspired by the US Constitution – Article 1, Section 3, Clause 1).

The only amendment to the 1891 Brazilian Constitution is from September 3, 1926, which altered articles 6, 34, 37, 59, 60, and 72. The modifications dealt with the Union's intervention in the States, the powers of the Congress, the President's veto power (who could now veto parts of a bill[2]), the powers of the Judiciary, the limitation of *habeas corpus* to violations of freedom of movement—suppressing the Brazilian doctrine of *habeas corpus* (Castro & Santos, 2021, p. 129), and clarified some fundamental rights, as well as specifying that there could be no tax exemptions due to the irreducibility of salaries.

2 The veto could be restricted to one word of the bill, such as for example "no," therefore substantively changing the meaning of the bill. This is clearly a problematic approach in the legislative process.

Amendments to a constitution are usually made to update and give them new life, so that they continue to govern the nation according to popular expectations. This was not the case with the single amendment to the 1891 Constitution. If the political climate in Brazil had already been deteriorating with the original text (Castro; Santos, 2021, p. 122), it was with the 1926 amendment that the system was pushed to its limits, with a significant increase in presidential powers to intervene in the states, while also granting the power of partial veto, which could truly reverse the meaning of legislation approved by Congress. Moreover, there was a reduction of the Judiciary's power, setting the stage for the so-called Revolution of 1930 just four years later. From the start, the 1926 reform didn't look promising, as it was approved under a state of siege (Hambloch, 2000, p. 89).

From then on, every subsequent constitution, with the exception of the 1988 Constitution, had a short life, the longest-lasting being the democratic Constitution of 1946 (21 years). Noteworthy is that the 1934 Constitution inaugurated an aspect of Brazilian constitutionalism: inserting the social dimension into its legal considerations. Since then, the length of constitutions has visibly increased, and the tradition started in 1934 was especially reinforced in the 1988 Constitution. From the 1934 Constitution on, civil family law (indissolubility of marriage), administrative law (especially concerning public servants), and economic order principles (social function of property), among others, were included in the constitutional text. It was also the first to provide for Electoral Justice, in article 82. Likewise, the position of Vice President of the Republic was suppressed, and the promulgation of laws when not done by the President of the Republic was assigned to the president of the Chamber of Deputies.

The method inaugurated for amending the 1934 Constitution, in art. 178 and paragraphs, can be summarized as follows: (i) the constitution could be altered by amendment or revision; (ii) an amendment could make changes that did not modify the State's political structure (arts. 1–14, and 17–21), or the organization and powers of the branches (chapters II, III, and IV, of Title I; chapter V of Title I; Titles II and III; and arts. 175, 177, 178, and 181); and (iii) a constitutional revision could alter what was not allowed to be changed by amendment.

The legislative process for constitutional amendments involved several stages. Initiatives could have been started either by one quarter of deputies or senators, or by a simple majority in more than half of state assemblies within two years. Deliberation required an absolute majority in both Houses—the Chamber of Deputies and the Senate—across two rounds per House each year, for two consecutive years. Alternatively, if any House approved an amendment by a two-thirds majority at any stage, the other House voted; if it also passed by two-thirds, the amendment was immediately promulgated.

For constitutional revisions, the process began with an initiative from two-fifths of deputies or senators, or by two-thirds of state assemblies acting by absolute majority. Approval by simple majority in both Houses resulted in a draft revision. During the next legislature, this draft had to pass three rounds of discussion and voting in both Houses over two consecutive years. While revisions incorporated their modifications directly into the constitution, amendments were appended at the end, following the model used in the United States.

Although it lasted only 3 years, the 1934 Constitution was amended once, through Legislative Decree No. 6 of 1935, which appended three modifications to the end of the constitutional text, under the name "amendments." Amendments 1, 2, and 3 to the 1934 Brazilian Constitution, promulgated by the Presidents and Secretaries of the Chamber of Deputies and Senate, addressed subversive acts. Amendment 1 allowed the President, with legislative approval, to declare a state of emergency for serious internal unrest. Amendment 2 permitted the Executive to strip military officers of rank and post for subversive actions, while Amendment 3 allowed the dismissal of civil servants for similar conduct, both subject to judicial review.

Thus, the logic of the 1934 Constitution's amendment system resumed the procedure adopted in the Imperial Constitution, placing modifications and additions at the end of the text, without altering the original wording. If they were revisions, the system was the same as in the 1891 Constitution, making changes in the body of the text, so that the original wording was lost.

Repeating the entrenched clause that began in the 1891 Constitution, the 1934 one also provided in its art. 178, § 5, that amendments or revisions tending to abolish the republican and federative form would not be admitted. On the other hand, and probably in reaction to how the 1926 amendment to the 1891 Constitution was approved, § 4 of art. 178 prohibited amending the constitution while a state of siege was in force.

It is worth noting that the Senate had been removed from the Legislative Power in the 1934 Constitution and did not formally belong to any of the Three Branches. Thus, the 1934 Constitution—in its Chapter V, Coordination of Powers—provided that it was up to the Senate "to promote the coordination of the federal powers among themselves, maintain administrative continuity, oversee the Constitution, collaborate in the making of laws, and perform other acts within its competence." Note that the constitution used the term "collaborate" with the Chamber of Deputies in making laws, since the Senate did not belong to the Legislative Branch, but, curiously, participated in the legislative process of enacting laws. Many of the powers attributed to the Senate in 1934 have been maintained throughout subsequent constitutions, including the 1988 Constitution.

In November 1937, Getúlio Vargas staged a coup d'état, imposing a new constitution on the country and shortening the life of the 1934 Constitution to just three years. The new constitutional regime was strongly inspired by the historical moment the world was experiencing, especially Europe. The rise of authoritarianism and extreme ideologies influenced Francisco Campos, the main author of the 1937 Constitution. Campos eventually defended his work by saying he was merely anticipating the legal system to what would inevitably prevail.

The 1937 regime abolished Electoral Justice, changed the name of the Senate to the Federal Council, instituted the National Economic Council (a normative and consultative body for labor and union relations), created decree-laws, and concentrated much more power in the hands of the President of the Republic. Article 73, for example, stated that The President of the Republic, supreme authority of the State, "coordinates the activities of the representative organs of higher degree, directs internal and external policy, promotes or guides national interest legislative policy, and supervises the administration of the Country." At the same time, the 1937 Brazilian Constitution maintained much of the structure of the 1934 Constitution, notably the articles and chapters on economic order, family, education, public servants, etc. (Macedo & Galvão, 2019, p. 195).

The 1937 Constitution was the first to mention that the President of the Republic could initiate the legislative process to amend the constitution. The procedure for amending the constitutional text was provided in art. 174, which used the term "constitutional law" to refer to the legislative instrument that carried constitutional reform, with the following wording: Art. 174 "The Constitution may be amended, modified, or reformed by initiative of the President of the Republic or the Chamber of Deputies."

With this wording, it reverted to the imperial system of only the Chamber of Deputies being able to initiate the amendment process (and the possibility of state assemblies proposing amendments was removed), but with the novelty that the President of the Republic could also do so.

Although the 1937 Constitution had an amendment procedure, it was never formally used. On the contrary, all reforms carried out to the 1937 Charter were made by constitutional laws issued solely by the President of the Republic at his exclusive discretion. Twenty-one constitutional laws were enacted. In fact, it was a true arbitrary and abusive use of the power to issue decree-laws, as provided in art. 180: "Until the national Parliament convenes, the President of the Republic shall have the power to issue decree-laws on all matters within the Union's legislative competence."

The Union's matters of competence were listed in art. 15, and there was no mention of the possibility of amending the Constitution in this article. All constitutional laws from this period were based on art. 180 to give a semblance of legality to something that was evidently unconstitutional. In fact, there was debate as to whether it was even possible to speak of a constitution in effect, since art. 187 required—for the effectiveness of the 1937 Charter—that a plebiscite be held, but it never occurred. Therefore, part of the doctrine of that time and even today says that the 1937 Constitution did not exist, it was merely a fiction (Siqueira, Amâncio & Marques, 2020, pp. 534–539). Siqueira et al. (2020, pp. 539–551) show that this common perception of the 1937 Constitution as not truly existing did not hold up in practice. During the authoritarian regime of 1937, many legal, statutory, and jurisprudential arguments were based on the constitutional text, and even daily life was influenced by it.

The constitutional laws sometimes amended the Constitution, and sometimes merely regulated matters autonomously. Of the 21 constitutional laws, twelve reformed the 1937 Constitution, three amended the Constitution by appending (American-style amendment), and six were scattered, i.e., they did not amend the Constitution, acting as truly autonomous laws. The laws are thus distributed by order number: Reform: nos. 1, 3, 5, 6, 7, 9, 10, 11, 12, 16, 17, 18; Appended: nos. 2, 4, 14; Scattered: nos. 8, 13 (calling the constituent assembly and returning the name Senate to the institution), 15, 19, 20, 21.

As can be seen, it was from the moment that amending the constitution became easier that the number of amendments to the fundamental law increased significantly compared to previous periods.

With Vargas's overthrow in October 1945 and the calling of a Constituent Assembly by Constitutional Law No. 13 of November 1945, a new constitution was drafted in September 1946. The 1946 Constitution, though not drafted based on a preliminary bill (Baleeiro & Sobrinho, 2012, p. 9), was quite similar to the 1934 one and brought back some provisions from 1891. Thus, in the 1946 regime, the Vice President of the Republic was reinstated as a substitute for the President and as president of the Senate. It was the first constitutional charter to expressly mention political parties and was amended 27 times.

From a legislative point of view, it was with amendment no. 4 of 1961 (establishing the parliamentary system of government) that the figure of the supplementary law was created[3], in its art. 22, as well as the figure of the delegated law, in the sole paragraph of the same article. With the repeal of amendment no. 4 and the return to the presidential system by amendment no. 6 of 1963, the constitutional basis for these types of laws formally disappeared, and only with amendment no. 17 of 1965 was the concept of supplementary laws resumed in Brazilian constitutionalism, although the 1946 Constitution still did not detail the approval process or the purpose of this type of law. Delegated laws did not return to the constitutional text after the repeal of amendment no. 4, only reappearing in the 1967 Constitution.

It was also on amendment no. 17 that was possible to delegate to special committees of the Senate or the Chamber of Deputies the capacity to consider and approve bills, which would be deemed approved by the respective House, what is today called the conclusive process in the internal regulations of the Senate and the Chamber of Deputies, respectively.

3 Two previous supplementary laws prior to 1961 were enacted, both from the State of Amazonas. These are supplementary laws no. 4 of 1947 and no. 25 of 1949, which dealt with the opening of additional credit. There is no indication that they served any function similar to the supplementary laws that emerged in 1961, but only a more thorough historical investigation could answer this question.

The amendment process was also a mix of 1934 and 1891, with the return of the initiative of state assemblies to propose amendments to the Constitution, and the removal of the President of the Republic's ability to initiate the legislative process of amendment. In summary, according to art. 217, the initiative to propose amendments to the Constitution could come from at least one quarter of the deputies or senators. Additionally, more than half of the state assemblies could also initiate the process; each assembly approved the proposal by a simple majority of its members within up to two years from the date of the first assembly's decision.

It would be approved if, alternatively, the proposal received an absolute majority of votes from both the Chamber of Deputies and the Senate, with two rounds of discussion and voting in each house across two consecutive ordinary legislative sessions. In the first session, there were two rounds in the Chamber of Deputies, while in the second session, two rounds took place in the Senate. Or received at least two-thirds of the votes in the Chamber of Deputies and Senate, in two rounds of discussion and voting, in which case it would not be necessary to wait for the interstice of one ordinary legislative session (approved by two-thirds in one House, it would be immediately submitted to the other's appreciation).

As in other republican constitutions, there were entrenched clauses for the federation and the republic. Similarly, it would not be possible to amend the constitution during a state of siege.

Paragraph 4 of art. 217 stated that the amendment approved by the Congress would be "attached" to the constitutional text, which might suggest that the incorporation method was appending, but several amendments approved during this period used the integrative method, blending the changes into the original text.

The 1946 Constitution would be effectively interrupted in 1964, with the military coup carried out by means of institutional acts, which had no legal or constitutional basis for their issuance. The first Institutional Act was issued on April 9, 1964, and it was followed by 17 additional institutional acts. The first of these had its preamble written by the Brazilian jurist Francisco Campos, the same author of the 1937 Constitution (Paixão, 2011, p. 158). The regime installed, seeking greater administrative capacity, promulgated a new constitution in 1967, which further concentrated powers in the Union, even allowing federal intervention in states that did not follow the federal government's economic and financial programs (art. 10, V, "c"). Likewise, the Supreme Court lost jurisdiction, and governors and secretaries of state accused of crimes against "national security" were judged by Military Justice. The Federal Justice was recreated, although no federal courts were provided for (except the two federal appellate courts), which existed in the regimes of 1891 and 1934.

Centralization could be seen even in the change of the title from "Federal Organization" to "National Organization," as happened in 1937 (Cavalcanti, Brito & Baleeiro, 2012, pp. 18–19). The concentration of powers in the President of the Republic was significant; the President not only had the exclusive capacity to initiate certain laws (as before), but it was also provided that Executive projects—when so requested—should be considered within a maximum of forty-five days, after which the respective projects would be considered approved if not deliberated by the Congress. In addition, legislative delegation to the Executive was maintained, as was the decree-law, which allowed the President of the Republic to issue decrees with the force of law, provided they dealt with national security or public finance, and they had to be approved by Congress within 60 days (parliamentary amendments were not allowed); if not deliberated in that period, they would be considered approved.

The legislative process for amendments described in the 1967 Charter is perhaps one of the simplest ever, stating in art. 50 that the constitution could be amended by initiative (i) of one quarter of senators or deputies; (ii) of the President of the Republic; or (iii) of more than half of the state assemblies, each expressing itself by absolute majority. There was an express provision that the states' proposal would be presented to the Senate.

Once received in the Chamber of Deputies or Senate, the proposal should be considered within 60 days, in two rounds of discussion and voting, being approved by an absolute majority of members of both Houses. Once approved, the amendment would be published by the Boards of the Chamber of Deputies and the Senate. There was no mention of the method of incorporation of amendments, and of the 27 amendments approved during this period, some were integrated into the text (e.g., amendments nos. 3, 4, 6, 10), while others were separate (e.g., amendments nos. 2, 12). Others were mixed (e.g., amendments nos. 5, 9, and 26, the latter calling the 1987 National Constituent Assembly). Three of the amendments were made by powers granted by institutional acts, those of nos. 1, 7, and 8.

A note should be made regarding Amendment No. 1 of 1969. Issued based on article 3 of Institutional Act No. 16, of October 1969, combined with § 1 of article 2 of Institutional Act No. 5, of December 1968, effectively granted by the military junta that governed the country in place of then President Costa e Silva, removed for health reasons (Cunha, 2023, p. 85). This amendment was actually a new constitution disguised as an amendment, as it altered a substantial part of the original text. In fact, in the whereas clauses of the amendment, there is a note of which articles were not altered and—in truth, something comical—it goes on to enumerate, in full, the 691 provisions not affected by the reform.

With the new wording, the procedure for approving amendments was slightly altered, keeping the same parties entitled to initiate, consideration, and promulgation, but altering the parliamentary initiative quorum from one quarter to one third of senators or deputies, as well as the approval quorum from absolute majority to two-thirds. Both the old and new wording provided for entrenched clauses of federation and republic, as well as prohibiting amendment of the constitution while a state of siege was in effect.

In the 1980s, Brazil went through a process of redemocratization[4]. Following amendment no. 26 in November 1985, the National Constituent Assembly met to draft a new constitution. In fact, this process began with Message No. 48/1985, from then President José Sarney, forwarding proposed constitutional amendment No. 43/1985, which became amendment no. 26. In the message, the President asked Congress to approve the proposed amendment because he believed the historical moment demanded that the authoritarian period be left

4 The long road that led to the Constituent Assembly can be traced back to the movements of July 1971, with the so-called "Carta de Recife" issued by the MDB. Starting in 1977, the idea of convening an exclusive constituent assembly gained more traction, even though it faced strong resistance from the military in government. Obstacles, such as the April Package, pushed the process of political opening further into the future, but also intensified the popular sentiment for a new constitution to be drafted. This history is detailed in the work of Leonardo Barbosa (2009). For more on this period prior to the drafting of the 1988 Constitution, see Paixão, 2011, p. 155, and Paixão; Carvalho, 2021.

behind and that the country move toward a Democratic State. After it was approved, Decree 91.450/1985 established the Provisional Commission for Constitutional Studies, the so-called Afonso Arinos Commission, which was tasked with drafting the constitutional bill. Composed of 50 jurists and chaired by Afonso Arinos de Melo Franco, its work did not serve as the basis for the 1988 Charter, which ended up being "built from the bottom up" (Paixão, 2011, p. 164).

The start of the work of the National Constituent Assembly (ANC) took place with the approval of the preliminary operating rules, through Resolution No. 1 of 1987, which provided for the schedule for drafting the ANC's Internal Regulations, speaking time, the Board, etc. Once approved, the internal regulations were enacted by Resolution No. 2 of 1987, when the constituent's work formally began.

Perhaps the aspect that most differentiated the drafting of the new constitution from the others was the degree of popular participation. A system was created whereby suggestions could be sent to the ANC to be analyzed and possibly incorporated into the final text. To facilitate the work, the Senate Data Processing Service (PRODASEN) established the Constituent Support Computer System (SAIC), which created a database with all suggestions received, totaling 72,719 popular submissions (Monclaire et al., 1991, p. 5).

The ANC operated from 1987 to 1988, when, on October 5 of that year, the new constitution was promulgated, being known as the "Citizenship Constitution". We will not dwell on a deeper analysis of the final text, as it will be addressed later in this work, but suffice it to say that the constitution followed much of what had already been done in others, dedicating chapters to social order, economic order, etc., as well as the traditional chapters describing the form of state and government, the exercise of powers, and so on.

Despite following traditions, there were also many innovations in this constitution, such as greater popular participation through the popular initiative for laws, plebiscite, and referendum; the autonomy of the Public Prosecutor's Office; the three-phase process of the public budget; the elevation of municipalities to the status of federative entities; the autonomy of the Federal District; the creation of the Superior Court of Justice (STJ), among others.

Within the Three Branches, the Executive retained the possibility of issuing acts with the force of law, no longer called decree-laws but provisional measures. Once issued, they must be immediately submitted to the Congress, and if not considered within 60 days, extendable for another 60, they will lose effectiveness (unlike decree-laws). Thus, the Legislature remained primarily responsible for legislating. But perhaps the branch most reformed was the Judiciary. The Supreme Court was given the power to declare laws and constitutional amendments unconstitutional, to declare the legislator in default for not enacting laws to enable the exercise of rights (and even issue a temporary injunction until Congress does so), among others.

For the first time, individual rights and guarantees were written at the beginning of the Charter, no longer at the end as in previous constitutions. Article 5 lists, in its 79 items, a wide range of rights, many of which already existed in past constitutions, but innovated by providing remedies to seek these rights in court. Thus, the legislator included in the constitution the classic *habeas corpus*, the writ of mandamus, and the new *habeas data* and writ of injunction, as well as the popular action—extended to cover administrative morality and environmental protection (Tácito, 2012, p. 22).

In the amendment process, there were no significant changes (not even the possibility of popular amendment proposals was added), essentially maintaining the same procedure as the 1967 Federal Constitution: the initiative to propose constitutional amendments could come from one third of senators or deputies, the President of the Republic, or from more than half of the state assemblies, each approving by a simple majority. The approval would be by the vote of three-fifths of senators and deputies, and two rounds of discussion and voting.

The 1988 Federal Constitution did not provide any method for incorporating amendments into the text, but in these more than 40 years, almost all types have been used.

There was, however, a substantial change in the scope of entrenched clauses. According to Paragraph 4 of art. 60, amendments proposals tending to abolish: (a) the federal form of the State; (b) direct, secret, universal, and periodic voting; (c) the separation of Powers; and (d) individual rights and guarantees should not be admitted, not even for discussion.

However, the Republic, which since 1891 had always been an entrenched clause, is no longer included in the prohibition. The most probable reason is that it was provided, in art. 2 of the Transitional Constitutional Provisions Act (ADCT), that a plebiscite would be held to choose the form of government (republic or monarchy) and the system of government (presidential or parliamentary). Although scheduled for September 7, 1993, it was actually held on April 21 of the same year, with the following results: 66% for republic; 10% for monarchy; 55.6% for presidentialism; 24.9% for parliamentarism.

Among the limitations on amendment power, in addition to the prohibition of amending the constitution under a state of siege, it is now also forbidden to amend the constitution under a state of defense or federal intervention.

In 2004, amendment number 45 created yet another type of amendment possibility in the 1988 Brazilian Constitution. International treaties and conventions approved by the Congress under the same procedure as constitutional amendments (two rounds, by three-fifths of the votes in each House) will be equivalent to amendments approved by the ordinary procedure. By 2025, the following treaties had been approved with amendment equivalence: International Convention on the Rights of Persons with Disabilities and its Optional Protocol, signed in New York on March 30, 2007; Marrakesh Treaty to Facilitate Access to Published Works for Persons Who Are Blind, Visually Impaired, or Otherwise Print Disabled, concluded under the World Intellectual Property Organization (WIPO), held in Marrakesh on June 27, 2013; Inter-American Convention against Racism, Racial Discrimination, and Related Forms of Intolerance, adopted in Guatemala during the 43rd Regular Session of the General Assembly of the Organization of American States, on June 5, 2013.

Having examined the evolution of the constitutional amendment process in Brazilian constitutions, we now turn to the analysis of other aspects of these constitutions in order to assess how they have changed, or not, over time.

Brazilian constitutional genealogies

The traditional theory of constituent power suggests that framers possess unlimited authority when establishing a new political consensus, envisioning a scenario where there is a complete break from past elements. However, historical evidence indicates that in practice, we experience "ruptures and continuities," meaning that remnants of past constitutional experiences are not entirely erased, as old constitutional practices persist in various forms. Mazzone and Tecimer (2022) introduce the concept of "interconstitutionalism" to illustrate how previous constitutions influence the interpretation and application of a new constitution. This discussion is also relevant in the realm of transitional justice, where the structures of the state of exception persist for a time due to the continued efficacy of sub-constitutional norms and judicial actions, even when a regime is radically and suddenly replaced (Pinheiro, 2019, pp. 207–208).

The present research does not seek to question the relevance of the constitutional process of 1988 and its innovations. Popular participation in the process from 1987 to 1988 is unprecedented in Brazilian history, given the pressure exerted by civil society, whose voice was repressed during the military dictatorship and craved for more space in the public sphere. Moreover, the Constituent Assembly's structure and organization had an original character, as it did not adopt a draft and organized the process in different phases (thematic committees, systematization committees, plenary and redaction committees), directly impacting the constitution's final text (Gomes, 2006).

Recent research in Brazilian constitutional history has uncovered the richness of pre-1988 constitutional experiences. Lynch and Mendonça (2017, p. 984) pointed out Brazilian constitutional history was long overlooked, with interpretations of the 1988 Constitution often being based on American and German theories. Besides that, some Brazilian authors called the pre-1988 period as the "Brazilian constitutional prehistory." Similarly, Barbosa (2009, p. 27–28) highlighted the arguments that sidelined Brazilian constitutional history, perceiving it as peripheral and fraught due to periods of exception. These authors refute these arguments, demonstrating the relevance and complexity of Brazilian constitutional history.

This research compares the texts of past Brazilian constitutions to identify persistent and changing elements over two hundred years of constitutional history. The data (constitutional texts) are organized and presented in tabular form to enable better visualization of specific information highlighting new research problems through juxtaposition. This initial survey is broad and panoramic, not centered on any specific theme.

Various research methods enhance our understanding of constitutional history. Analyzing only the constitutional text is insufficient; one must also consider the shaping debates, the political context, and the different uses of constitutional semantics. Constructing Brazilian historiography requires many contributors, and the diverse research methods and perspectives of individual researchers lead to a more precise and sophisticated understanding of this constitutional journey. When comparing constitutions, it is crucial to avoid superficial understandings of words and expressions, as their meaning change over time and can be disputed even within the same period, especially for concepts like "democracy" and "republic." Political battles often occur in the semantic field, making the compilation and comparison of different Brazilian constitutional texts valuable for research focused on the "history of concepts."

This detailed comparison of all Brazilian constitutional texts can enhance existing analyses and provide material for future research, such as establishing parallels between the 1934 and 1988 Constitutions (Cepêda, 2013). The choice of terms and expressions in different constitutions holds meaning; despite shifts in meaning over time, the deliberate repetition of words across regimes is a conscious choice, possibly to reframe their significance or because their meanings are already established for those drafting a new Fundamental Charter. In other words, when incorporating provisions from past constitutions, the constituent does so not capriciously but because they recognize the appropriate political and legal value in these older texts, which should be preserved.

A notable characteristic of Brazilian constitutional history is how each new regime often builds upon the framework of its predecessor. This analysis does not intend to undermine the historical context or dismiss the work of historiographers in Brazil. Instead, it highlights how successive Brazilian constitutions have frequently incorporated provisions from earlier ones, with remarkable consistency and intensity.

For historical context, Figure 1.1 presents a timeline of Brazil's constitutions and their durations. The longest-lasting were the 1824 Imperial Constitution and the 1891 First Republican Constitution, while the 1934 Constitution was the shortest-lived, lasting only three years. Despite its brief existence, the 1934 Constitution significantly influenced the texts of later constitutions, including the current 1988 Constitution.

To understand the origins of the 1988 Constitution, a data survey was conducted to compare different constitutions. This work was

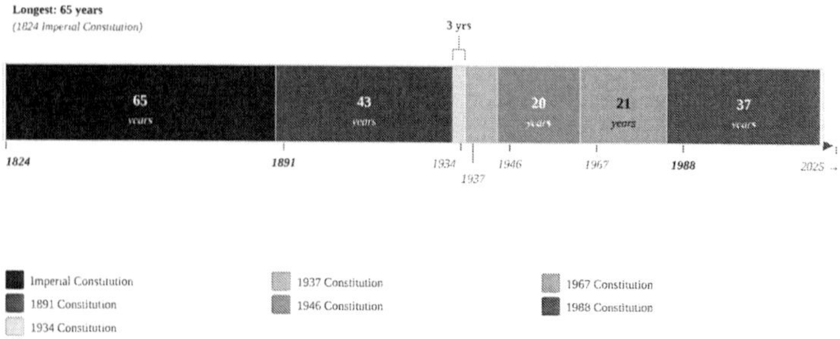

Figure 1.1 Timeline of national constitutions, with their age in years.

motivated by the discovery that many provisions in the 1988 Federal Constitution closely resemble or are even identical to those in earlier constitutions. For example:

- 1891 Constitution: Article 72, § 22: "Habeas corpus shall be granted whenever someone suffers or is in imminent danger of suffering violence through illegal imprisonment or constraint on their freedom of movement."
- 1934 Constitution: Article 113, 23: "Habeas corpus shall be granted whenever someone suffers or is threatened with violence or coercion on their freedom due to illegality or abuse of power. It does not apply to disciplinary infractions."
- 1937 Constitution: Article 122, 16: "*Habeas corpus* shall be granted whenever someone suffers or is in imminent danger of suffering illegal violence or coercion in their freedom of movement, except in cases of disciplinary punishment."
- 1946 Constitution: Article 141, § 23: "*Habeas corpus* shall be granted whenever someone suffers or is threatened with violence or coercion on their freedom of movement due to illegality or abuse of power. It does not apply to disciplinary infractions."
- 1967 Constitution: Article 150, § 20: "*Habeas corpus* shall be granted whenever someone suffers or is threatened with violence or coercion on their freedom of movement due to illegality or abuse of power. It does not apply to disciplinary infractions."
- 1969 Constitutional Amendment No. 1: Article 153, § 20: "*Habeas corpus* shall be granted whenever someone suffers or is threatened with

violence or coercion on their freedom of movement due to illegality or abuse of power. It does not apply to disciplinary infractions."

- 1988 Constitution: Article 5, LXVIII: "*Habeas corpus* shall be granted whenever someone suffers or is threatened with violence or coercion on their freedom of movement due to illegality or abuse of power."

The texts of different Brazilian constitutions show a remarkable similarity, often nearly identical in wording. This doesn't mean the application of *habeas corpus* has always been as comprehensive as it is today. Instead, it shows that this provision has appeared in multiple constitutions with nearly the same wording, as if unchanged.

This repetition isn't rare. A survey for this chapter found numerous constitutional provisions with similar patterns, making it a notable feature of Brazilian constitutionalism. For example:

- 1891 Constitution: Article 15. The organs of national sovereignty are the Legislative, Executive, and Judiciary, harmonious and independent from each other.
- 1934 Constitution: Article 3. The organs of national sovereignty, within constitutional limits, are the Legislative, Executive, and Judiciary, independent and coordinated among themselves.
- 1946 Constitution: Article 36. The powers of the Union are the Legislative, Executive, and Judiciary, independent and harmonious among themselves.
- 1967 Constitution: Article 6. The powers of the Union, independent and harmonious, are the Legislative, Executive, and Judiciary.
- 1969 Constitutional Amendment No. 1: Article 6. The powers of the Union, independent and harmonious, are the Legislative, Executive, and Judiciary.
- 1988 Constitution: Article 2. The powers of the Union, independent and harmonious among themselves, are the Legislative, Executive, and Judiciary.

And:

- 1891 Constitution: Article 38. If the law is not promulgated within 48 hours by the President of the Republic in the cases of §§ 2 and 3 of Article 37, the President of the Senate, or the Vice-President, if the former does not do so within the same period, shall promulgate it using the following formula: "F., President (or Vice-President) of the Senate, hereby inform those who see this that the Congress decrees and promulgates the following law (or resolution)."

- 1934 Constitution: Article 46. If the law is not promulgated within 48 hours by the President of the Republic in the cases of §§ 1 and 2 of Article 45, the President of the Chamber of Deputies shall promulgate it using the following formula: "The President of the Chamber of Deputies hereby announces that the Legislative Power decrees and promulgates the following law."
- 1946 Constitution: Article 70, § 4. If the law is not promulgated within 48 hours by the President of the Republic in the cases of §§ 2 and 3, the President of the Senate shall promulgate it; and if the latter does not do so within the same period, the Vice-President of the Senate shall do it.
- 1967 Constitution: Article 62, § 4. If the law is not promulgated within forty-eight hours by the President of the Republic in the cases of §§ 2 and 3, the President of the Federal Senate shall promulgate it; and if the latter does not do so within the same period, the Vice-President of the Federal Senate shall do it.
- 1969 Constitutional Amendment No. 1: Article 59, § 5. If the law is not promulgated within forty-eight hours by the President of the Republic in the cases of § 2 and § 3, the President of the Federal Senate shall promulgate it; and if the latter does not do so within the same period, the Vice-President of the Federal Senate shall do it.
- 1988 Constitution: Article 66, § 7. If the law is not promulgated within forty-eight hours by the President of the Republic in the cases of § 3 and § 5, the President of the Senate shall promulgate it, and if the latter does not do so within the same period, it shall be the responsibility of the Vice-President of the Senate to do it.

These examples illustrate a recurring pattern in our constitutions. The reuse of past provisions in new texts can be motivated by both practical reasons, when drafting a constitution is based on a previous model, given the extensive topics covered, and political reasons, where assembly members may wish to retain provisions that align with their interests. Nevertheless, it is remarkable how new charters often draw from their predecessors, reintroducing past provisions. It is almost as if they form a single constitution, repeatedly modified over more than a century, with the 1988 Charter being the latest iteration.

The Ship of Theseus paradox, which questions whether an object remains the same when all its parts are replaced or if it becomes something new, is relevant to this discussion. The paradox, derived from the myth of Theseus, the founder of Athens, poses the question: if all parts of Theseus's ship, which the Athenians preserved in his honor, are replaced over time, is it still the same ship? Hobbes adds another layer to the paradox: if someone rebuilt the ship with the old parts, which would be the true ship of Theseus—the old or the new? (Hobbes, 1656, p. 100).

This thought experiment relates to our topic. If many parts of old constitutions are included in new ones, to what extent does the constitution retain the essence of the old? While the old charter has no legal force, it highlights the legal-political choice to incorporate elements of old constitutions into new ones. We propose the term "constitutional transference" to describe this phenomenon.

When a law from the old regime is applied to the new regime, either fully or partially, it is referred to as "reception." This process is assumed for all laws and can be reviewed by the Supreme Court when necessary. However, when provisions are incorporated into the new constitutional text, it is not reception because the reference norm is the constitution itself. A term was needed to describe this phenomenon, even if initially for educational purposes.

"Transference" can be either semantic, when the idea of the old provision is mostly or entirely transferred to the new text, or literal, when the old provision is included in the new text in identical or nearly identical terms, as shown in previous examples. To determine the extent of this transference in the 1988 Federal Constitution and understand its historical foundations, a table was created showing the genealogy of provisions in the current 1988 Constitution. Due to its size, only excerpts are provided here for illustration.

In this table, provisions from old constitutions are grouped with those in the new constitution, tracing their historical origins. In some cases, the provisions differ more significantly, with the old ones being only ideologically similar to the current ones but still addressing the same topic (Table 1.1).

In other instances, the old provisions can gradually set the course that will lead to the current form (Table 1.2).

Table 1.1 Articles about "culture" in Brazilian constitutions

Federal Constitution 1891	*Federal Constitution 1934*	*Federal Constitution 1937*	*Federal Constitution 1946*	*Federal Constitution 1967*	*CA nº 1 of 1969*	*Federal Constitution 1988*
	CHAPTER II OF EDUCATION AND CULTURE	OF EDUCATION AND CULTURE	CHAPTER II OF EDUCATION AND CULTURE	TITLE IV OF FAMILY, EDUCATION AND CULTURE	TITLE IV OF FAMILY, EDUCATION AND CULTURE	SECTION II Culture
Art 35. It is incumbent, furthermore, upon Congress, but not exclusively: 2nd) to encourage within the Country the development of literature, arts, and sciences (...)	Art. 148. It is incumbent upon the Union, the States, and the Municipalities to foster and stimulate the development of science, arts, literature, and general culture, protect objects of historical interest and the artistic heritage of the Country, as well as provide assistance to the intellectual worker.	Art 128 - Art, science, and teaching are free to the initiative of individuals, associations, and public and private corporate entities. It is the duty of the State to contribute, directly and indirectly, to the stimulation and development of them (art, science, and teaching), by favoring or founding artistic, scientific, and educational institutions.	Art 173. The sciences, literature and the arts are free. Art 174. The State has a duty to support culture.	Art 171. The sciences, literature and the arts are free. Sole paragraph. The Public Authorities shall encourage scientific and technological research. Art 172. The State has a duty to support culture.	Art. 179. The sciences, literature and the arts are free, subject to the provisions of paragraph 8º of Article 153. Sole paragraph. The Public Authorities shall encourage scientific and technological research and education. Art. 180. The State has a duty to support culture.	Article 215. The State shall ensure to everyone the full exercise of cultural rights and access to sources of national culture and shall support and foster the appreciation and diffusion of cultural expressions.

Table 1.2 Articles about "public service" in Brazilian constitutions

Imperial Constitution 1824	*Federal Constitution 1891*	*Federal Constitution 1934*	*Federal Constitution 1937*	*Federal Constitution 1946*	*Federal Constitution 1967*	*CA n° 1 of 1969*	*Federal Constitution 1988*
Art. 179, XIV. Every citizen can be admitted to Civil, Political, or Military Public Offices, without distinction that doesn't arise out of his talents, and virtues.	Art. 73. Civil, or military, public offices are accessible to all Brazilians, if it be met the conditions of special capacity established by law, paid accumulations of office notwithstanding.	Art. 168. Public offices are accessible to all Brazilians, without distinction of sex or marital status, if it be met the requirements established by law.	Art. 122, 3. Public offices are equally accessible to all Brazilians, if it be met the conditions of capacity prescribed by law and regulation.	Art. 184. Public offices are equally accessible to all Brazilians, if it be met the requirements established by law.	Art. 95. Public offices are accessible to all Brazilians, given they meet the requirements established by law.	Art. 97. Public offices are accessible to all Brazilians who meet the requirements established by law.	Art. 37, I. Public offices, positions and functions are accessible to all Brazilians who meet the requirements established by law, as well as to foreigners, as provided by law.

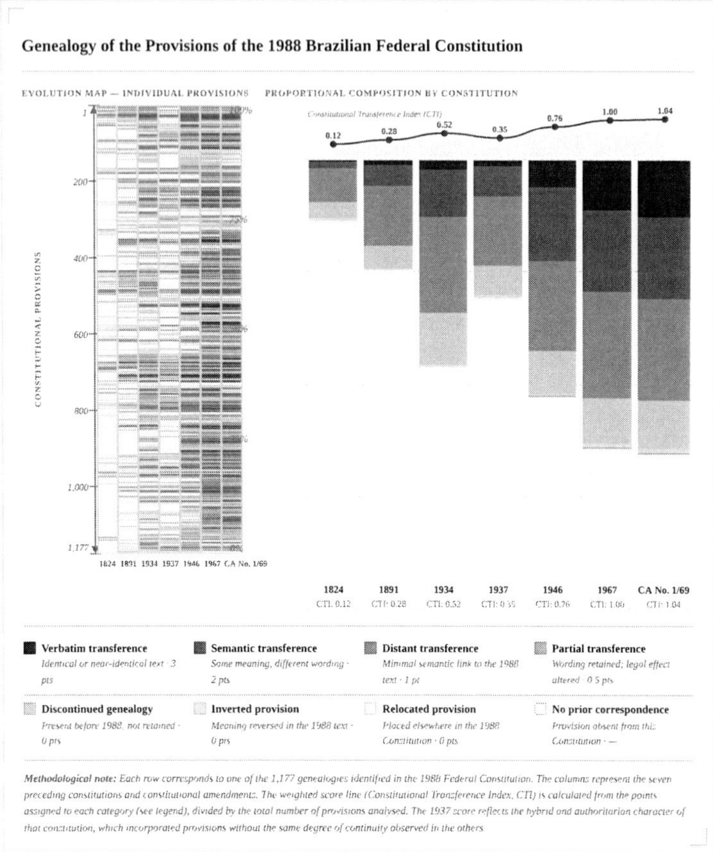

Figure 1.2 Simplified version of the table of Constitutional genealogies.

Considering this scenario, given the large number of provisions to be analysed, the following methodology was adopted. Each provision was classified according to its degree of proximity to the form it assumed in 1988, and points were assigned accordingly. In Figure 1.2, these categories are rendered in a greyscale ordered by score, from near-black (strongest continuity) to near-white (absence)::

- Verbatim transference (near-black): literal equality or nearly so—there may be one or two word changes, for example—in relation to the form in which the provision exists in the 1988 text (3 points).

- Semantic transference (dark grey): very close or identical semantic proximity, but with different wording (2 points).
- Distant transference (medium grey): minimal or low semantic equality, but with a clear relationship to the ancestry of the current provision (1 point).
- Partial transference (medium-light grey): provisions that were "recycled", where part of the text was retained but something essential was changed, altering the legal effect it produces. For instance, a legislative procedure that previously allowed automatic approval once the deadline expired, but which no longer results in automatic approval, while still preserving the original process (0.5 points).
- Discontinued genealogy (light grey): provisions whose genealogy was abandoned in 1988 (zero points).
- Inverted provision (pale grey): provisions whose sense was reversed when incorporated into the 1988 Constitution—for example, something previously permitted became prohibited in the current Federal Constitution (zero points).
- Relocated provision (very light grey): provisions that no longer have a counterpart in 1988 but are described in another part of the current text—for example, a competence originally inscribed in one article and now described elsewhere, interrupting the genealogy of the first provision (zero points).
- Cells left blank (near-white) indicate that the provision had no correspondence in that constitution.

Table 1.3 provides some examples of this classification scheme.

Similarly, when a particular constitution adds a new genealogy to constitutional history, it gains an additional point beyond what it would be entitled (beyond what it is shown in the classification above). For instance (Table 1.4), the 1891 Constitution created a new lineage of provisions with its Article 63. As a result, it was classified as medium green (2 points) and also earned an extra point for being the first in the lineage of the genealogy of Article 25 of the 1988 Federal Constitution, totaling 3 points.

Using these criteria, we classified all identified genealogies. However, it is important to acknowledge the inherent subjectivity in any legal classification, especially when interpreting provisions and assessing their similarity. Different readers may have varying perspectives on the classification method used here, which is a natural

Table 1.3 Comparison between Brazilian constitutions

Imperial Constitution 1824	*Federal Constitution 1891*	*Federal Constitution 1934*	*Federal Constitution 1937*
POLITICAL CONSTITUTION OF THE EMPIRE OF BRAZIL	CONSTITUTION OF THE REPUBLIC OF THE UNITED STATES OF BRAZIL	CONSTITUTION OF THE REPUBLIC OF THE UNITED STATES OF BRAZIL	CONSTITUTION OF THE UNITED STATES OF BRAZIL
Art. 1. The EMPIRE of Brazil is the Political association of all Brazilian Citizens. They form a free, and independent, Nation, which doesn't accept any bond whatsoever of union, or federation, that conflicts with its independence. Art. 2. Its territory is divided into Provinces in the form in which it is currently found, which can be subdivided, such as is needed for the good of the State. Art. 3. Its Government is Monarchical-Hereditary, Constitutional and Representative.	Art. 1° The Brazilian Nation adopts as a form of government, under the representative regime, the Federative Republic proclaimed on November 15, 1889, and is constituted, by perpetual and indissoluble union of its former provinces, in the United States of Brazil.	Art. 1.° The Brazilian Nation, constituted by the perpetual and indissoluble union of the States, the Federal District and the Territories in the United States of Brazil, maintains as a form of government, under the representative regime, the federative Republic proclaimed on November 15, 1889.	Art 1° Brazil is a republic. Political power emanates from the people and is exercised in their name and in the interest of their well-being, their honor, their independence and their prosperity. Art. 3°. Brazil is a federal state, constituted by the indissoluble union of the States, the Federal District and the Territories. Its current political and territorial division is maintained.
Art. 12. All the aforementioned Powers in the Empire of Brazil are delegations of the Nation.		Art. 2. All power emanates from the people and will be exercised in their name.	

Federal Constitution 1946	*Federal Constitution 1967*	*CA nº 1 of 1969*	*Federal Constitution 1988*
CONSTITUTION OF THE UNITED STATES OF BRAZIL	CONSTITUTION OF BRAZIL	CONSTITUTION OF THE FEDERATIVE REPUBLIC OF BRAZIL	CONSTITUTION OF THE FEDERATIVE REPUBLIC OF BRAZIL
Art. 1º The United States of Brazil maintains, under the representative regime, the Federation and the Republic. All power emanates from the people and will be exercised in their name. § 1º The Union comprises, in addition to the States, the Federal District and the Territories. § 2º The Federal Distric is the Capital of the Union.	Art. 1º - Brazil is a Federative Republic, constituted, under the representative regime, by the permanent union of the states, the Federal District and the Territories.	Art. 1º. Brazil is a Federative Republic, constituted, under the representative regime, by the permanent union of the states, the Federal District and the Territories.	Article 1. The Federative Republic of Brazil, formed by the permanent union of the states, the municipalities, and the Federal District, is a democratic State ruled by the law and founded on: I – sovereignty; II – citizenship; III – human dignity; IV – social values of labor and free enterprise; V – political pluralism.
	§ 1º - All power emanates from the people and will be exercised in their name.	§ 1º All power emanates from the people and will be exercised in their name.	Sole paragraph. All power emanates from the people, who exercise it by means of elected representatives or directly, as provided under this Constitution

(*Continued*)

Table 1.3 (Continued)

Imperial Constitution 1824	*Federal Constitution 1891*	*Federal Constitution 1934*	*Federal Constitution 1937*
Art. 9. The Division, and harmony of the Political Powers is the chief conserver principle of the Citizens Rights, and surest means of making effective the guarantees that the Constitution offers. Art. 10. The Political Powers recognized by the Constitution of the Empire of Brazil are four: the Legislative, the Moderator, the Executive and the Judicial.	Article 15. The organs of national sovereignty are the legislative, the executive, and the judicial branch, which are independent and harmonious with each other.	Article 3. The organs of national sovereignty are, within the constitutional limits, the legislative, the executive, and the judicial branch, which are independent and coordinated with each other.	
		CHAPTER I Political Rights	Nationality and Citizenship
Art. 90. The appointments of Deputies, and Senators for the General Assembly, and Members of the General Councils of the Provinces, will be made by indirect Elections, the group of active Citizens in Parish Assemblies electing the Provincial Voters, and these the Representatives of the Nation, and Province.		Article 108. Can be voters brazilians of both sexes, over 18 years old, who enlist in the form of the law.	Art. 117 - Electors are those Brazilians of either sex, over eighteen years of age, who register in accordance with the law and are in the full enjoyment of political rights

Federal Constitution 1946	*Federal Constitution 1967*	*CA nº 1 of 1969*	*Federal Constitution 1988*
Article 36. The powers of the Union are vested in the legislative, the executive, and the judicial branch, which are independent and harmonious with each other.	Article 6 - The powers of the Union,which are independent and harmonious, are vested in the legislative, the executive, and the judicial branch.	Article 6. The powers of the Union,which are independent and harmonious, are vested in the legislative, the executive, and the judicial branch.	Article 2. The powers of the Union are vested in the legislative, the executive, and the judicial branch, which are independent and harmonious with each other.
CHAPTER I Nationality and Citizenship	CHAPTER II Political Rights	CHAPTER II Political Rights	CHAPTER IV Political Rights
Art 131 - Electors are those Brazilians over eighteen years of age who register in accordance with the law. Art 134 - Suffrage is universal and direct; the vote is secret; and the proportional representation of national political parties is ensured, in the manner established by law.	Art 142 - Electors are those Brazilians over eighteen years of age, registered in accordance with the law. Art 143 - Suffrage is universal and the vote is direct and secret, except for the cases provided for in this Constitution; the proportional representation of political parties is ensured, in the manner established by law.	Art. 147. Electors are those Brazilians over eighteen years of age, registered in accordance with the law. Art. 148. Suffrage is universal and the vote is direct and secret, except for the cases provided for in this Constitution; political parties shall have proportional representation, total or partial, in the manner established by law.	Article 14. The sovereignty of the people shall be exercised by universal suffrage and by direct and secret voting, with equal value for all and according to the law, by means of: (...)

(*Continued*)

Table 1.3 (Continued)

Imperial Constitution 1824	*Federal Constitution 1891*	*Federal Constitution 1934*	*Federal Constitution 1937*
Art. 91. Have a vote in these primary elections: I. Brazilian Citizens, who are in the enjoyment of their political rights. II. Naturalized foreigners.		Article 109. Voter registration and voting are mandatory for men and for women, when the latter exercise a remunerated public office, subject to the sanctions and exceptions that the law shall determine.	
Art. 92. Are excluded from voting in the Parish Assemblies:	Art. 70, § 1° Cannot be enlisted as voter for federal elections, or for those of the States:	Art. 108, Sole paragraph. Cannot register as voter:w	
	1° The beggars	c) the beggars;	
	2° The illiterate;	a) the illiterate;	
	3° The enlisted ranks, except for the students of military schools of higher education;	b) the enlisted ranks, except for the sergeants, from the Army or the Navy and the auxiliary forces of the Army, as well as the students of military schools of higher education and the cadets;	

Federal Constitution 1946	*Federal Constitution 1967*	*CA n° 1 of 1969*	*Federal Constitution 1988*
Art 133 - Registration and voting are mandatory for Brazilians of both sexes, except for the exemptions provided by law.	§ 1° - registration and voting are mandatory for Brazilians of both sexes, except for the exemptions provided by law.	§ 1° Registration and voting are mandatory for Brazilians of both sexes, except for the exemptions provided by law.	Paragraph 1. Electoral enrollment and voting are: I – mandatory for people over eighteen years of age; II – optional for: a) the illiterate; b) those over seventy years of age; c) those over sixteen and under eighteen years of age.
Art 132 - The following cannot register as electors:	§ 3° - The following cannot register as electors:	§ 3° The following shall not be permitted to register as electors:	Paragraph 2. Foreigners, and conscripts during their period of compulsory military service, are forbidden to register as voters.
I - the illiterate;	a) the illiterate;	a) the illiterate;	

(*Continued*)

Table 1.3 (Continued)

Imperial Constitution 1824	*Federal Constitution 1891*	*Federal Constitution 1934*	*Federal Constitution 1937*
IV. The Religious, and anyone, who live in a claustral Community.	4º The religious of monastic orders. companies, congregations, or communities of any denomination, subject to a vote of obedience, rule, or statute, which implies the renunciation of individual freedom.	d) those who are temporarily or permanently deprived of political rights.	
I. Those under twenty-five years old, in which the married are not included, and Military Officers, who are over twenty-one years old, the Graduate Bachelors, and Clergy of Sacred Orders.			Art. 117, The military in active duty, except the officers, who cannot be voters.

Federal Constitution 1946	*Federal Constitution 1967*	*CA n° 1 of 1969*	*Federal Constitution 1988*
III - those who are temporarily or permanently deprived of political rights.	c) those who are temporarily or permanently deprived of political rights.	c) those who are temporarily or permanently deprived of political rights.	
II - those who cannot express themselves in the national language;	b) those who cannot express themselves in the national language;	b) those who cannot express themselves in the national language; and	
Sole Paragraph. Military personnel are eligible to register as voters, provided that they are officers, officer cadets, midshipmen, sub-lieutenants or sub-officers, sergeants, or students of military higher education schools for officer training.	Art. 142, § 2.º - Military personnel are eligible to register as voters, provided that they are officers, officer cadets, midshipmen, sub-lieutenants or sub-officers, sergeants, or students of military higher education schools for officer training.	§ 2º Military personnel are eligible to register as voters, provided that they are officers, officer cadets, midshipmen, sub-lieutenants or sub-officers, sergeants, or students of military higher education schools for officer training.	

Table 1.4 Provisions on state constitutions in Brazilians Federal Constitutions

Imperial Constitution 1824	*Federal Constitution 1891*	*Federal Constitution 1934*	*Federal Constitution 1937*	*Federal Constitution 1946*	*Federal Constitution 1967*	*CA nº 1 of 1969*	*Federal Constitution 1988*
CHAPTER V Of the General Councils of Province, and their attributions.	CHAPTER III The States	-	-	-	CHAPTER III Of the Competence of States and Municipalities	CHAPTER III OF THE STATES AND MUNICIPALITIES	CHAPTER III The Federated States
-	Art. 63. Each State shall be governed by the Constitution and the laws it adopts, respecting the constitutional principles of the Union.	Art. 7º. It is the exclusive responsibility of the States: I - decree the Constitution and the laws by which they are to be governed, respecting the following principles:	Art. 21. It is the exclusive responsibility of the State: I - decree the Constitution and the laws by which they should be governed;	Art 18. Each State will be governed by the Constitution and the laws it adopts, observing the principles established in this Constitution.	Art 13. States are organized and governed by the Constitutions and laws they adopt, observing, among other principles established in this Constitution, the following:	Art. 13. States will organize and be governed by the Constitutions and laws they adopt, respected among other principles established in this Constitution, the following:	Article 25. The states are organized and governed by the Constitutions and laws they may adopt, in accordance with the principles of this Constitution.

variation in legal sciences. The goal is not to provide mathematically precise results but to offer a reasonably clear presentation of the collected data. With these considerations in mind, let us examine the results.

Figure 1.2 presents the results in two complementary panels. On the left, the Evolution Map offers a simplified version of the complete table of genealogies: each of its 1,177 rows corresponds to one provision of the 1988 Constitution, and each column to one of the seven preceding constitutional texts, from 1824 to Constitutional Amendment No. 1 of 1969. On the right, stacked bars show the proportional composition of each constitution by category of transference, surmounted by the Constitutional Transference Index (CTI), the weighted average of the points assigned under the criteria above.

The image clearly shows more blank cells in the initial columns and greater density, with progressively darker shading and fewer blanks, in the final columns (a movement mirrored in the steady rise of the CTI across the series). This indicates that once provisions were incorporated into constitutions, most were not removed and remained in subsequent texts. This trend demonstrates a growing consensus among different generations of constitutional drafters that certain past provisions should be included in the new charters they composed. The sole deviation from this trajectory is the 1937 Constitution, whose lower score reflects its hybrid and authoritarian character, breaking the continuity otherwise observed across the series.

After assigning weights to all points, the sum of these points was calculated for each constitution. We call this result the "proximity index," which measures how closely each provision aligns —either literally or semantically—with its counterpart in the 1988 Brazilian Constitution. The results are presented in Table 1.5.

The 1967 Federal Constitution has the highest proximity index of 1296.5. While this might suggest that the 1988 Charter closely resembles the constitution from the 1964 regime, it is important to consider two key factors.

First, using the previous text as a starting point for drafting the current constitution is a common practice in both national and global constitutionalism (Lynch & Mendonça, 2017, p. 1000; Mazzone & Tecimer, 2022, p. 348). The 1967 text served as a foundation, with necessary changes incorporated for the new regime.

Second, the constitution's text alone does not determine the nature of a regime—whether it is democratic or autocratic; historical context

Table 1.5 Proximity index of the Brazilian constitutions

1824 Constitution	*1891 Constitution*	*1934 Constitution*	*1937 Constitution*	*1946 Constitution*	*1967 Constitution*	*Amendment 1 – 1969*
260	478	835	431	977	1269.5	1249

is crucial. For example, the Imperial Constitution of 1824 granted extensive powers to the emperor, leading to political clashes under Dom Pedro I, who eventually abdicated. In contrast, his son, Dom Pedro II, used these powers more moderately, maintaining stability during the Second Reign (Bonavides, 2000, p. 170). Similarly, the 1946 Constitution, enacted by an elected constituent assembly and seen as a return to democracy after the "Estado Novo," was disregarded by the Military Dictatorship starting in 1964. The dictatorship bypassed its rules through seventeen institutional acts, even amending the constitution illegally. Similarly, the 1937 Charter, nicknamed "A Polaca," was sidelined by Vargas himself. He ruled through decrees and constitutional laws, ignoring the plebiscite provision in the *Magna Carta* of that time (Siqueira, Amâncio, & Marques, 2020, pp. 534–539).

An authoritarian government can render a democratic constitution ineffective, while a democratic regime can remove autocratic elements from an old constitution to support democratic rule. Rather than imitating the 1967 Charter, the 1988 Federal Constitution uses it as a starting point due to its temporal proximity. As illustrated in Figure 1.2, Brazil often utilizes past texts as foundations for new ones. Notably, the 1988 Charter had no preliminary draft, as the *Arinos Commission*'s work was waived by the Federal Government (Arantes & Couto, 2006, p. 60).

The perception that constituent work in Brazil is done incrementally, with past constitutions serving as building blocks for subsequent ones, is reinforced by the increasing indices over time, except in 1937, which will be discussed later.

To gain a clearer understanding of each constitution's impact, another table focuses on the new elements introduced by each charter. This analysis, referred to as the "novelty index," calculates points solely for inaugurating new genealogies—one point each—without considering any other factors. The 1891 Federal Constitution is the only one scoring in this methodology, while the others have no points.

This approach allows for the identification of which constitutions introduced the newest genealogies and had the greatest influence on the 1988 Constitution. The results are shown in Table 1.6.

Interestingly, this metric reveals a reversal. The 1934 Federal Constitution ranks first, followed by the 1891 Constitution, then the 1824 Constitution, and finally the 1967 Charter. The 1934 Constitution, despite lasting only three years, significantly influenced the current constitution. The 1891 Constitution, as the first republican

Table 1.6 Constitutions that inaugurated new themes and most impacted the text of the 1988 Constitution

1824 Constitution	*1891 Constitution*	*1934 Constitution*	*1937 Constitution*	*1946 Constitution*	*1967 Constitution*	*Amendment 1 – 1969*
117	150	219	17	84	116	30

constitution, also had a major impact. Surprisingly, the 1824 Imperial Constitution, Brazil's first constitution, ranks third, having introduced several key provisions that persist until today.

To understand why the 1967 Charter ranks fourth in terms of novelty, we can analyze which themes each constitution influenced the most. By summing up the genealogical contributions of each title, chapter, section, etc., in the 1988 Federal Constitution, we identify the points with the highest levels of novelty. Table 1.7 shows this analysis using percentage values to indicate each constitution's contribution to that genealogy. For instance, 66.7% of the genealogy of the Fundamental Principles was inaugurated by the Imperial Constitution.

Initially, it's evident that the first three columns contain darker colors, indicating a higher number of significant indices. Conversely, the last three columns have a larger portion of lighter colors, demonstrating lower indices. Thus, it's clear that the first three constitutions had the most influence on the text of the 1988 CF.

The three most influenced themes (with at least two points) by each constitution are summarized below:

- 1824 Constitution:
  - Regarding individual and collective rights and duties: 20 points
  - Regarding the president's duties: 14 points
  - Regarding the Congress's duties: 7 points
- 1891 Constitution:
  - Regarding intervention: 13 points
  - Regarding the national tax system: 12 points
  - Regarding the president's responsibility: 11 points
- 1934 Constitution:
  - Regarding the Union: 27 points
  - Regarding individual and collective rights and duties: 12 points
  - Regarding electoral courts and judges: 12 points
  - Article 7 (workers' rights): 10 points
  - Regarding the national tax system: 10 points
  - Regarding education, culture, and sports: 10 points
- 1937 Constitution:
  - Article 7 (workers' rights): 2 points
  - Regarding the union: 2 points
  - Article 23 (common competence of federal entities): 2 points

Table 1.7 Percentage values to indicate each Constitution's contribution to that genealogy

1824	*1891*	*1934*	*1937*	*1946*	*1967*	*CA nº 1/69*	*Federal Constitution of 1988*
66.7%	33.3%	0.0%	0.0%	0.0%	0.0%	0.0%	Title I – Fundamental Principles
44.4%	20.0%	26.7%	0.0%	6.7%	2.2%	0.0%	Title II – Fundamental Rights and Guarantees
0.0%	0.0%	55.6%	11.1%	22.2%	11.1%	0.0%	Art. 7º (workers rights)
41.7%	0.0%	33.3%	0.0%	0.0%	25.0%	0.0%	Chapter III – Nationality
31.6%	21.1%	26.3%	0.0%	21.1%	0.0%	0.0%	Chapter IV – Political Rights
0.0%	0.0%	0.0%	0.0%	12.5%	87.5%	0.0%	Chapter V – Political Parties
11.1%	55.6%	11.1%	11.1%	0.0%	11.1%	0.0%	Title III – The Organization of the State
4.1%	18.4%	55.1%	4.1%	4.1%	12.2%	2.0%	Chapter II – The Union
0.0%	29.4%	47.1%	11.8%	11.8%	0.0%	0.0%	Art. 23 (collective power of the federal entities)
42.9%	28.6%	0.0%	0.0%	0.0%	14.3%	14.3%	Chapter III – The Federated States
12.5%	25.0%	25.0%	0.0%	0.0%	0.0%	37.5%	Chapter IV – The Municipalities
0.0%	25.0%	0.0%	0.0%	0.0%	75.0%	0.0%	Chapter V – The Federal District and the Territories
0.0%	61.9%	9.5%	0.0%	9.5%	9.5%	9.5%	Chapter VI – Intervention
7.1%	7.1%	28.6%	0.0%	14.3%	35.7%	7.1%	Chapter VII – Public Administration
0.0%	9.1%	36.4%	0.0%	54.5%	0.0%	0.0%	Section II – Government Employees
66.7%	22.2%	0.0%	0.0%	11.1%	0.0%	0.0%	Chapter I – The Legislative Power & Section I – The National Congress
24.1%	34.5%	31.0%	0.0%	0.0%	0.0%	10.3%	Section II – Powers of the National Congress
75.0%	0.0%	25.0%	0.0%	0.0%	0.0%	0.0%	Section III – The Chamber of Deputies
54.5%	27.3%	18.2%	0.0%	0.0%	0.0%	0.0%	Section IV – The Federal Senate
9.1%	18.2%	31.8%	0.0%	18.2%	13.6%	9.1%	Section V – Deputies and Senators
0.0%	20.0%	20.0%	10.0%	40.0%	0.0%	10.0%	Section VI – The Sessions & Section VII – The Committees

14.6%	17.1%	4.9%	2.4%	12.2%	41.5%	7.3%	Section VIII – The Legislative Process
0.0%	18.2%	27.3%	0.0%	9.1%	36.4%	9.1%	Section IX – Accounting, Financial and Budgetary Control
7.7%	61.5%	15.4%	0.0%	7.7%	0.0%	7.7%	Chapter II – The Executive Power
53.8%	15.4%	11.5%	0.0%	7.7%	7.7%	3.8%	Section II – Duties of the President of the Republic
0.0%	84.6%	7.7%	7.7%	0.0%	0.0%	0.0%	Section III – Liability of the President of the Republic
60.0%	0.0%	40.0%	0.0%	0.0%	0.0%	0.0%	Section IV – The Ministers of State
0.0%	0.0%	75.0%	0.0%	0.0%	25.0%	0.0%	Section V – The Council of the Republic and the National Defense Council
30.0%	0.0%	60.0%	0.0%	10.0%	0.0%	0.0%	Chapter III – The Judicial Power
17.6%	17.6%	52.9%	0.0%	0.0%	5.9%	5.9%	Art. 95 (Judges' guarantees), Art. 96 (exclusive competencies of the courts), Art. 100 (court ordered payments)
19.0%	33.3%	28.6%	4.8%	14.3%	0.0%	0.0%	Section II – The Supreme Federal Court
9.1%	18.2%	45.5%	0.0%	9.1%	18.2%	0.0%	Section III – The Superior Court of Justice
0.0%	22.7%	31.8%	4.5%	31.8%	0.0%	9.1%	Section IV – The Federal Regional Courts and the Federal Judges
0.0%	0.0%	11.1%	0.0%	44.4%	44.4%	0.0%	Section V – Labour Courts and Judges
0.0%	0.0%	80.0%	0.0%	20.0%	0.0%	0.0%	Section VI – Electoral Courts and Judges
0.0%	37.5%	25.0%	0.0%	0.0%	37.5%	0.0%	Section VII – Military Courts and Judges
25.0%	0.0%	25.0%	0.0%	50.0%	0.0%	0.0%	Section VIII – Courts and Judges of the States
0.0%	33.3%	33.3%	0.0%	33.3%	0.0%	0.0%	Section I – The Public Prosecution & Section II – The Public Advocacy

(*Continued*)

Table 1.7 (Continued)

1824	*1891*	*1934*	*1937*	*1946*	*1967*	*CA nº 1/69*	*Federal Constitution of 1988*
14.3%	21.4%	35.7%	7.1%	7.1%	14.3%	0.0%	Section II – The State of Siege
54.5%	0.0%	45.5%	0.0%	0.0%	0.0%	0.0%	Chapter II – The Armed Forces
0.0%	0.0%	20.0%	0.0%	0.0%	80.0%	0.0%	Chapter III – Public Security
2.1%	25.5%	21.3%	0.0%	8.5%	36.2%	6.4%	Chapter I – The National Tax System
0.0%	0.0%	0.0%	0.0%	36.4%	63.6%	0.0%	Section VI – Tax Revenue Sharing
0.0%	7.7%	30.8%	3.8%	0.0%	50.0%	7.7%	Section II – Budgets
0.0%	4.8%	33.3%	4.8%	23.8%	23.8%	9.5%	Title VII – The Economic and Financial Order
50.0%	0.0%	33.3%	0.0%	16.7%	0.0%	0.0%	Title VIII – The Social Order
12.5%	6.3%	62.5%	0.0%	18.8%	0.0%	0.0%	Chapter III – Education, Culture and Sports
0.0%	25.0%	50.0%	25.0%	0.0%	0.0%	0.0%	Section II – Culture
0.0%	20.0%	60.0%	20.0%	0.0%	0.0%	0.0%	Chapter VII – Family, Children, Adolescents, Young People and the Elderly

- 1946 Constitution:
  - Regarding regional federal courts and federal judges: 7 points
  - Regarding public servants: 6 points
  - Regarding the legislative process: 5 points
  - Regarding the economic and financial order: 5 points
- 1967 Constitution:
  - Regarding the legislative process: 17 points
  - Regarding the national tax system: 17 points
  - Regarding budgets: 13 points
- CA nº 1/69:
  - Regarding municipalities: 3 points
  - Regarding the powers of the Congress: 3 points
  - Regarding the legislative process: 3 points
  - Regarding the national tax system: 3 points
  - Regarding intervention: 2 points
  - Regarding deputies and senators: 2 points
  - Regarding regional federal courts and federal judges: 2 points
  - Regarding budgets: 2 points
  - Regarding the economic and financial order: 2 points.

The 1967 Constitution introduced major innovations, primarily in the tax and budgetary areas. These lineages accounted for 63% of the topic of Tax Revenue Allocation and 50% of the Budget topic in this constitution, and they also inaugurated 36% of the provisions related to the National Tax System. Furthermore, the 1967 Constitution significantly influenced the legislative process, with the wording and organization of the introductory part almost entirely repeated in the 1988 Constitution (Table 1.8).

The 1967 Constitution also introduced many provisions related to Political Parties and Public Security. This explains its relatively high level of novelty, even though it ranks fourth. When combined with proximity indices, these data show that the 1967 Constitution served more as a textual starting point for the 1988 Constitution than having a significant influence. The most important constitutions for our current regime are, in order, the 1934, 1891, and 1824 Constitutions.

Despite its low novelty index (only 84), the 1946 Constitution is also significant, with a high proximity index (977). Additionally, the 1946 Charter revived some institutions from the 1891 Constitution.

The constitutions of the 1930s had a certain experimental character, introducing some changes that were later reversed. In 1891, the

Table 1.8 Comparison between Constitutional articles on legislative process

Federal Constitution of 1967	*CA nº 1 of 1969*	*Federal Constitution of 1988*
SECTION V The Legislative Process Art 49 - The legislative process comprises the preparation of:	SECTION V The Legislative Process Art. 46. The legislative process comprises the preparation of:	SECTION VIII The Legislative Process Article 59. The legislative process comprises the preparation of:
I – Amendments to the Constitution;	I – Amendments to the Constitution;	I – Amendments to the Constitution;
II – supplementary laws;	II – supplementary laws;	II – supplementary laws;
III – ordinary laws;	III – ordinary laws;	III – ordinary laws;
IV – delegated laws;	IV – delegated laws;	IV – delegated laws;
V - law-decree;	V - law-decree;	V – provisional presidential decrees;
VI – legislative decrees;	VI – legislative decrees; and	VI – legislative decrees;
VII – resolutions.	VII – resolutions.	VII – resolutions.

Congress was established, continuing the Empire's bicameral system with the Chamber of Deputies and an upper chamber renamed the Federal Senate. Similarly, the Federal Supreme Court (successor to the Imperial Supreme Court) and the Federal Judiciary system were created. In 1934, the Congress was abolished, leaving only the Chamber of Deputies in the Legislative Branch. The Senate gained a coordinating role among the branches of government. Under the 1937 regime, the Federal Judiciary was abolished, and the former Senate (now renamed as the Federal Council) returned to the Legislative Branch, remaining one of the Houses of the National Parliament, not the Congress. Only in 1946 did all these institutions revert to their initial configuration from 1891, with a Congress composed of the Chamber of Deputies and the Senate, and the Supreme Court serving as the apex body of the reestablished Federal Judiciary system. Additionally, the Federal Appeals Court was created as the second instance of the Union's judiciary.

In 1988, some of the functions of the Federal Appeals Court (TFR) were transferred to the newly established Superior Court of Justice

(STJ), while the remaining functions were assigned to the newly created Regional Federal Courts (TRF).

The 1946 Constitution was also the first to acknowledge that the Court of Auditors of the Union (TCU) assists the Congress in overseeing the Union's financial administration. The TCU was established in 1891, initially known simply as the Court of Auditors, and it succeeded the former National Treasury Court (as provided in the Imperial Constitution). Through Law No. 23, dated October 30, 1891, the responsibilities of the National Treasury Court were transferred to the Court of Auditors:

> Article 12. The following is abolished within the Ministry of Finance:
>
> b) The National Treasury Court, as soon as the Court of Auditors is established, transferring to the latter the responsibilities of judgment previously assigned to the former. The purely consultative or administrative functions of the ex tinct corporation now fall under the authority of the Minister of Finance, who will handle matters with individual or collective hearings involving the respective directors.

From the beginning, the Court of Auditors was much more associated with its financial function than with assisting the Congress. Although the TCU was moved to the Legislative Branch in the constitutional topography in 1967, it was in 1946 that it became closely connected to the Congress as an auxiliary in the external control function.

Finally, it was with the 1946 Federal Constitution that the Labor Justice became part of the Judiciary (despite having been created in the 1934 Constitution), previously being an organ of the Executive Branch (Morel & Pessanha, 2007, p. 91).

However, it is the triad 1824–1891–1934 Constitutions that truly shaped the current constitutional framework, as these three constitutions contributed the most to the country's fundamental legal structure. The 1891 Constitution established the foundations of the state model still in use today—later restored in 1946—including a federal republic with powers exercised by the Congress, the President of the Republic, and the Supreme Court, as well as the division into Union, states, and municipalities. The 1891 Constitution also introduced rules regarding intervention and states of siege, as well as the secular nature of the State.

The 1934 Constitution, beyond expanding the Union's competencies as delineated in Article 5, inaugurated the social and economic orders, as well as sections pertaining to family, education, and culture, among other provisions that remain relevant today. The Imperial Constitution, which established the constitutional framework of the nascent independent Brazilian state, was primarily responsible for laying the foundational principles (still applicable today) for citizenship and nationality regulations, as well as individual rights and guarantees.

In summary, we can deduce that the 1967 Federal Constitution—in conjunction with its Amendment No. 1 of 1969—may have played a role in shaping the language, serving as a starting point for the 1988 project (in addition to its budgetary and tax aspects). However, the most significant antecedents for the current constitutional regime appear to be the first three constitutions. To simplify, the 1824 Constitution provided the substratum, the 1891 Constitution laid the foundations, and the 1934 Constitution served as the mold; while the 1946 Constitution functioned as the preliminary draft that ultimately led to the 1988 Federal Constitution.

Final considerations

After briefly mentioning the history of amendment process, especially in the US, this chapter explored the transformations in Brazilian constitutions since 1824, including the different procedures adopted in those constitutions regarding amendments. By looking at Brazilian history, it was possible to track down the continuing process of establishing a procedure for amending the constitution. Therefore, the 1988 Brazilian constitution rules of amendment were fabricated and tested long before that.

This chapter explored not only the amendment procedures, but also other substantive matters. Acknowledging that the Constitutions of 1824, 1891, and 1934 played a pivotal role in shaping our contemporary regime seems crucial for a proper interpretation of the guiding principles of the Brazilian current constitution. Studying and comprehending the 1988 Federal Constitution, therefore, extends beyond the period of 1987–1988 or even the preceding military dictatorship. Instead, it involves observing the long constitutional development that spans from the Empire (from 1822 to 1889) to the early republican constitutions, with their specific terminologies and linguistic nuances.

Moreover, the struggle for the realization of rights in Brazil often hinges on the reiteration of provisions across various constitutions, attempting to concretize them within the new regime. This phenomenon is evident, for instance, in the case of *habeas corpus*. If the Republic's Constitution has deeper historical roots than previously postulated, a more thorough examination of these roots becomes essential for a more comprehensive understanding of this significant work. The metaphor of the Cathedral is useful in the sense that it highlights this long-term construction of a constitution that is not ever finished.

In this manner, the present endeavor seeks to fortify the existing body of research that contemplates constitutional history from a more interconnected perspective, thereby examining the way various constitutions resonate with one another. In the case of Brazil, these arguments may serve as an additional element for a broad discussion on the origins and roots of the current 1988 Constitution.

References

Ackerman, B., & Katyal, N. (1995). Our unconventional founding. *University of Chicago Law Review*, 62(2), 475–573.

Albert, R. (2018). Constitutional amendment and dismemberment. *Yale Journal of International Law*, 43(1), 1–84. Retrieved from https://openyls.law.yale.edu/bitstream/handle/20.500.13051/6721/RichardAlbertConstitution.pdf

Arantes, R. B., & Couto, C. (2006). Constituição, governo e democracia no Brasil. *Revista Brasileira de Ciências Sociais*, 21(61), 41–62. https://doi.org/10.1590/S0102-69092006000200003

Baleeiro, A., & Sobrinho, B. L. (2012). *1946* (3rd ed.). Brasília: Senado Federal.

Barbosa, L. A. de A. (2009). *Mudança constitucional, autoritarismo e democracia no Brasil pós-1964* (Doctoral dissertation, Universidade de Brasília). https://repositorio.unb.br/bitstream/10482/4075/1/2009_LeonardoAugustodeAndradeBarbosa.pdf

Bonavides, P. (2000). A evolução constitucional do Brasil. *Estudos Avançados*, 14(40), 155–176. https://doi.org/10.1590/S0103-40142000000300016

Castro, T. de S., & dos Santos, G. F. (2021). A revisão constitucional de 1926 e a tutela dos direitos individuais: Um ensaio sobre os efeitos da limitação do habeas corpus na prática jurisprudencial do STF. *Revista História do Direito,* 2(3), 118–142. https://doi.org/10.5380/hd.v2i3.83092

Cavalcanti, T. B., de Brito, L. N., & Baleeiro, A. (2012). *1967* (3rd ed., Vol. 6). Brasília: Senado Federal.

Cepêda, V. A. (2013). As constituições de 1934 e 1988: Trajetória histórica e inflexão política. *Cadernos do Desenvolvimento*, 8(12), 269–283. Retrieved from www.cadernosdodesenvolvimento.org.br

Cunha, B. (2023). The codification of constitutional amendments in Brazil: Beyond the appendative and integrative models. In R. Albert (Ed.), *The architecture of constitutional amendments: History, law, politics* (pp. 75–88). Oxford: Hart Publishing.

de Macedo, J. A. C., & Galvão, L. M. (2019). O novo Estado e o projeto de futuro da Constituição de 1937. In Arilda Arboleya, Hilton Costa, Jonas Wilson Pegoraro, Ana Lúcia Pretto Pereira (eds.). *Futuro do pretérito: O Brasil segundo suas constituições* (pp. 187–206). Curitiba: Appris Editora. https://www.amazon.com.br/Futuro-Pret%C3%A9rito-Brasil-Segundo-Constitui%C3%A7%C3%B5es-ebook/dp/B086R6MCLS

Gomes, S. (2006). O impacto das regras de organização do processo legislativo no comportamento dos parlamentares: Um estudo de caso da Assembleia Nacional Constituinte (1987–1988). *Dados – Revista de Ciências Sociais*, 49(1), 193–224.

Hambloch, E. (2000). *Sua majestade o presidente do Brasil: Um estudo do Brasil constitucional (1889–1934)*. Brasília: Senado Federal.

Hobbes, T. (1656). *Elements of philosophy: The first section, concerning body*. London: Printed by R. & W. Leybourn for Andrew Crooke. Retrieved from https://archive.org/details/b30335838

Holton, W. (2008). *Unruly Americans and the origins of the constitution*. New York, NY: Hill and Wang.

Klein, C. (1978). Is there a need for an amending power theory? *Israel Law Review*, 13(2), 203–214.

Laskar, M. E. (2013). *Summary of social contract theory by Hobbes, Locke, and Rousseau*. https://dx.doi.org/10.2139/ssrn.2410525

Lindseth, P. L. (2004). The paradox of parliamentary supremacy: Delegation, democracy, and dictatorship in Germany and France, 1920s–1950s. *Yale Law Journal*, 113, 1341–1415.

Lutz, D. S. (1994). Toward a theory of constitutional amendment. *American Political Science Review*, 88(2), 355–370. https://doi.org/10.2307/2944709

Lynch, C. E. C., & de Mendonça, J. V. S. (2017). Por uma história constitucional brasileira: Uma crítica pontual à doutrina da efetividade. *Revista Direito & Práxis*, 8(2), 974–1007.

Mazzone, J., & Tecimer, C. (2022). Interconstitutionalism. *Yale Law Journal*, 132, 326–398.

Monclaire, S., Magalhães, M. I., Filho, C. de B., & Impelizieri, F. (1991). *A constituição desejada: SAIC—As 72.719 sugestões enviadas pelos cidadãos*

brasileiros à Assembleia Nacional Constituinte (Vol. 1). Brasília: Senado Federal.
Morel, R. L. M., & Pessanha, E. G. da F. (2007). A justiça do trabalho. *Tempo Social,* 19(2), 87–109.
Nogueira, O. (2012). *1824* (3rd ed., Vol. 1). Brasília: Senado Federal.
Ostrom, V., & Allen, B. (2008). *The political theory of a compound republic: Designing the American experiment*. Lanham, MD: Lexington Books.
Paixão, C. (2011). Direito, política, autoritarismo e democracia no Brasil: Da Revolução de 30 à promulgação da Constituição de 1988. *Araucaria: Revista Iberoamericana de Filosofía, Política y Humanidades*, 13(26), 146–169. Retrieved from https://revistascientificas.us.es
Paixão, C., & Carvalho, C. P. (2021). História do Direito: RHD. *História do Direito: RHD*, 2(3), 300–319.
Pinheiro, D. A. R. (2019). O constitucionalismo espectral: Presença, tempo e narrativa à luz de Roque Larraquy. *Revista de Direitos e Garantias Fundamentais*, 20(3), 199–224.
Roznai, Y. (2013). Unconstitutional constitutional amendments: The migration and success of a constitutional idea. *American Journal of Comparative Law*, 61(3), 657–720.
Siqueira, G. S., Amâncio, G. C. de O., & Marques, F. M. M. (2020). A "constituição esquecida": O tratamento histórico da Constituição de 1937 nos livros de direito constitucional. *Revista Argumentum*, 21(2), 531–559.
Tácito, C. (2012). *1988* (3rd ed., Vol. 7). Brasília: Senado Federal.

2 The stability of the constitution in its quantitative aspect

Introduction

The objective of this chapter is to clarify is the practical implications of numerous amendments on the stability of the constitutional text. As previously noted, there is a pervasive argument that our constitution appears fragile or ineffective due to its accumulation of amendments.

However, the sheer quantity of amendments should not necessarily indicate political dysfunction.[1] Switzerland has amended its constitution almost every year since 1999, totaling 49 amendments.[2] The German constitution has been subject to amendments more than 60 times since 1949. Analogously, the Austrian constitution has undergone a little more than 140 amendments since 1920.[3] Austrian jurists even acknowledge that the actual number could be much higher, possibly reaching hundreds of changes, leading local doctrine to describe it as a "shattered" and "failed" constitution (Stelzer, 2013, p. 9).

These cases underscore that the frequency of amendments alone does not inherently signify dysfunction but rather reflects the dynamic nature of constitutional development.

1 "Contemporary societies are complex, so the demand for decisions is much greater today than at the time when the constitution was invented as a thing. Of course, from the point of view of the legislative process, it is possible to criticize the options made explicit by the derived constituent, but the amount of amendments should not be seen, by itself, as an intrinsic problem or a sign of concern" (Paixão, 2011, p. 166).

2 Swiss Confederation, *Federal Constitution of the Swiss Confederation of April 18, 1999 – Chronology*, source: www.fed lex.admin.ch/ eli/cc/1999/404/it/history

3 Republic of Austria, Federal Constitutional Act, source: https://www.ris.bka.gv.at/GeltendeFassung.wxe?Abfrage=Bundesnormen&Gesetzesnummer=10000138

DOI: 10.4324/9781003679202-3

Correspondingly, a salient argument has been raised here that the mere numerical quantity does not necessarily denote either the significance of the various changes or imply that the Brazilian constitution was completely rewritten. A striking exemplification of this is Amendment No. 1 of 1969, which, despite being a single amendment, was responsible for almost entirely rewriting the 1967 Constitution.

Given these considerations, let us analyze the amendments from a quantitative perspective. To ascertain the stability of an article, we observed the frequency of its amendments. Logically, an article subject to frequent alterations exhibits low stability, as successive reforms suggest that, at least from a political standpoint, it may be inadequate. Again, if the constitution's perceived weakness stems from its high rate of change, the same principle applies to its constituent articles.

Methodology

The **crystallization index** and **crystallization rate** are designed to assess the stability of specific sections of the constitution over time. To grasp this concept more intuitively, consider the following analogy: Suppose that instead of having 132 amendments dispersed throughout the entire constitutional text, all of them were concentrated in a single article. It would become apparent that this article is problematic. In fact, it might even warrant removal from the constitution, given that the rest of the articles remain unchanged and, therefore, stable—indicating no political controversy or need for modification.

Now, imagine that over 100 amendments affect not just one article but three or four. Once again, these frequently amended articles would demonstrate low stability, while the untouched articles would show maximum stability. In these examples, it becomes clear that the problem lies not in the total number of amendments but in the fact that certain articles are problematic, while most of the constitution remains intact.

This leads to the need for a deeper understanding of how the amendments have impacted the constitution as a whole. Are the changes distributed across many sections, or are they concentrated in just a few articles? Ultimately, how stable is the current Constitution? To assess this, two measures have been developed: the crystallization index and the crystallization rate.

The term "crystallization" refers to how stable—or "crystallized"—a specific article or section of the constitution is. The more an article has been amended over the years, the less stable (or less crystallized) it becomes. This analysis focuses on the number of amendments, which may invite criticism since the quantity of amendments does not necessarily reflect their significance or quality. However, this metric responds to arguments that the Constitution has lost its effectiveness due to the sheer number of amendments. A qualitative assessment of the amendments will follow, but for now, this metric serves to address concerns about the frequency of changes. A comprehensive investigation was conducted into all amendments up to the conclusion of 2025, encompassing a total of 138 constitutional amendments.

Crystallization index and rate

Two metrics are used to measure stability: the **crystallization index** and the **crystallization rate**.

- **Crystallization Index**: This index is calculated using a simple formula: the age of the Constitution (37 years, as of 2025) minus the number of amendments an article has received. The maximum possible index for 2025 is 37, meaning an article that has never been amended will have the highest crystallization index, indicating maximum stability. The more amendments an article has, the lower its index, signifying lower stability. However, the maximum possible value of the index changes as the Constitution ages, making direct comparison across different years difficult. To account for this, the **crystallization rate** normalizes[4] the measurement.
- **Crystallization Rate**: The rate is calculated by dividing the number of amendments by the age of the article and subtracting this from 1. This result gives the percentage of amendments relative to the article's age, which is then multiplied by 10 to yield the crystallization rate. The formula can be expressed as follows:

$$\textit{Crystallization Rate} = (1 - \textit{Number of Amendments} / \textit{Age of the Article}) \times 10$$

4 Normalization is a data processing and statistics technique used when you want to place a data set with variable values within the same scale, which can be [-1,1] or [0.0,1.0], etc. (Han, Kamber, & Pei, 2012, pp. 113–114). In our work, we use the normalization of the type Min-Max.

This method ensures that stability can be measured consistently over time, providing a clearer picture of how various sections of the Constitution have evolved and how stable they remain today.

The rate is at its maximum when it equals 10 (light green color) and at its minimum when it equals 0 (red color). The legend and color gradient can be found in the respective appendices (see below). For example:

- Article 5, two amendments (no. 45, of 2004 and 115, of 2022):
  - Index: 37 − 2 = 32
  - Rate: (1 − (2/37)) × 10 = 9.4

In addition to allowing the normalization of the measurement, the rate also enables better calculation of the crystallization of articles created after 1988. Since the index has the age of the Constitution as its maximum value, newer articles would have a distorted crystallization measurement, as they themselves are not 34 years old. The distortion is smaller in articles that are from after 1988 but are already old (10 or 20 years old), which is why they were included in the crystallization index measurement. However, articles that are one or two years old, for example, were excluded, as the rate measurement proves to be more suitable.

Analysis

The methodology has been explained in Introduction section. All the data is summarized in Table 2.1.

As evidenced, the preponderance of articles in the Constitution demonstrates high levels and crystallization rates (predominantly green). Given that most articles have been amended only a few times, the seemingly high number of total amendments becomes diffused throughout the text, which itself encompasses many more articles than there are amendments. While there are concentration points that may indicate potential issues, the remaining articles have undergone few amendments over their lifespan.

When considering only the crystallization index, a greater number of articles are depicted in black or darker shades of grey. This is attributable to the scale of this measure being relative to the lifespan of the Constitution, with the lowest value representing the lowest crystallization observed across all articles. This approach facilitates a

Table 2.1 Simplified version of Appendix D

Arts. 1–33	Arts. 34–67	Arts. 68–101	Arts. 102–131	Arts. 132–163	Arts. 163A–187	Arts. 188–219	Arts. 219A–250
1	34	68	102	132	163-A	188	219-A
2	35	69	103	133	164	189	219-B
3	36	70	103-A	134	164-A	190	220
4	37	Art. 37	103-B	135	165	191	221
5	38	72	104	136	166	192	222
6	39	73	105	137	166-A	193	223
7	40	74	106	Art. 167	167	194	224
8	41	75	107	139	167-A	195	225
9	42	76	108	140	167-B	196	226
10	43	77	109	141	167-C	197	227
11	44	78	110	142	167-D	198	228
12	45	79	111	143	167-E	199	229
13	46	80	111-A	144	167-F	200	230
14	47	81	112	145	167-G	201	231
15	48	82	113	146	168	202	232
16	49	83	114	146-A	169	203	233
17	50	84	115	147	170	204	234
18	51	85	116	148	171	205	235
19	52	86	117	149	172	206	236
20	53	87	118	149-A	173	207	237
21	54	88	119	150	174	208	238
22	55	89	120	151	175	209	239
23	56	90	121	152	176	210	240
24	57	91	122	153	177	211	241
25	58	92	123	154	178	212	242
26	59	93	124	155	179	212-A	243
27	60	94	125	156	180	213	244
28	61	95	126	157	181	214	245
29	62	96	127	158	182	215	245-A
29-A	63	97	128	159	183	216	246
30	64	98	129	160	184	216-A	247
31	65	99	130	161	185	217	248
32	66	100	Art. 100	162	186	218	249
33	67	101	131	163	187	219	250

← lower index = more modified

Crystallisation Index scale

Index 25 (Rate 7.4) — *Index 34 (Rate 10.0)*

New provision (Index 0)

■ Art. 37 — Public Administration
■ Art. 167 — Budgetary Restrictions
■ Art. 100 — Court-Ordered Payments

Note: *Each cell represents one article of the 1988 Constitution. Background shading encodes the crystallisation index (0–34): the number of constitutional comparisons in which the article was preserved unchanged, normalised to a 0–10 rate (Rate = Index × 10/34). Darker cells indicate more frequent modification; lighter cells indicate greater textual stability. Mid-grey cells (Index = 0) denote provisions added after 1988 with no historical comparator. Articles are arranged in eight groups of 34, reading left to right and top to bottom from Art. 1 (upper-left) to Art. 250 (lower-right). Art. 37 (Public Administration) and Art. 167 (Budgetary Restrictions) record the lowest index (25), denoting maximum modification. Source: Appendix D.*

relative classification, enabling us to comprehend how the stability of individual articles compares to one another.

In this regard, the articles that warrant attention are 21, 29, 37, 40, 42, 100, 155, 159, 167, and 198, which address the following subjects:

- Article 21 (7 amendments): Union prerogatives,
- Article 29 (5 amendments): provisions regarding the election of mayors and vice mayors, the number of councillors in municipal chambers, and councillors' remuneration;

- Article 37 (9 amendments): general provisions of Public Administration;
- Article 40 (6 amendments): social security for public servants;
- Article 42 (5 amendments): military personnel of states, the Federal District, and territories;
- Article 100 (7 amendments): precatory orders;
- Article 155 (5 amendments): state and Federal District taxes;
- Article 159 (5 amendments): distribution of tax revenues;
- Article 167 (9 amendments): restrictions in budget laws;
- Article 198 (6 amendments): guidelines for the Unified Health System (SUS), rules for minimum investment in public health, and minimum wage for healthcare professionals.

The low stability of these articles suggests that the subject matter they address could potentially be the purview of ordinary law, or at the very least, complementary law (except for Union competencies, which must be enshrined in the Constitution due to federal issues). This assertion stems from the fact that these matters are evidently revisited frequently by Parliament, which sound legislative practice dictates that such frequently modified provisions are better relegated to laws (as is the case, for example, with budget laws).

However, these articles alone account for a small proportion of the amendments, as can be observed in Table 2.2. It is evident that forty percent of the Constitution, nearly half, remains unaltered. Of the remainder, almost thirty percent, has been modified once, and half of that has been modified up to twice. Therefore, 113 articles have been modified at most twice, representing 47.7% of the constitution's articles (which is nearly the other half).

These data corroborate the findings illustrated in Table 2.2: a significant portion of the articles in the Constitution exhibits stability, either because the articles have not been amended or because they have been modified very infrequently. The articles with low stability (problematic, so to speak) account for a mere 3.6% of the total (ten articles), which is a minuscule quantity compared to the 271 articles that comprise the Constitution.

Indeed, Appendix D reveals a significant dispersion of amendments throughout the table, indicating their well-distributed presence within the constitutional text. Notably, not only have a few articles undergone extensive modifications to the Constitution, but this has also

Table 2.2 Percentage of modified and non-modified articles in the 1988 Constitution

Unmodified	116 articles	42.8%
Modified up to once	72 articles	26.6%
Modified up to twice	41 articles	15.1%
Modified up to three times	15 articles	5.5%
Modified up to four times	16 articles	5.9%
Modified up to five times	4 articles	1.5%
Modified up to six times	2 articles	0.7%
Modified up to seven times	2 articles	0.7%
Modified up to eight times	0 articles	0%
Modified up to nine times	2 articles	0.7%

occurred over a relatively short span of years. At the end of Appendix D there are the total modifications for each year, as in, for example, the years of 1998 (51 modifications), 2003 (25 modifications), 2004 (30 modifications), 2019 (25 modifications), 2021 (23 modifications), and 2022 (21 modifications).

In particular, 1998 marked the year of the administrative reform carried out by Amendment No. 19/98, while 2004 witnessed the judicial reform enacted by Amendment No. 45/04. Conversely, over a span of six years, no modifications occurred, whereas in 17 years, there were five changes or fewer, for instance. With an average of 9.6 modifications per year across 37 years, 22 years (65%) fall below this average.

Employing the data from Appendix D, it is feasible to construct Table 2.3 containing the crystallization indices and their corresponding percentages.

These results reinforce the findings demonstrated in Table 2.2: slightly over forty percent of the constitution exhibits maximum crystallization (or stabilization). Despite the proximity of this data, it is essential to distinguish between mere modification and crystallization. The former measures only the absolute value of changes, whereas the latter considers the age of the article alongside the changes. An article that has been amended nine times in nine years will have very low crystallization, whereas an article amended nine times in one hundred years will exhibit extremely high crystallization.

Table 2.3 Crystallization indices and their corresponding percentages

Index	*Percentage*
34	44.6%
33	20.7%
32	14.4%
31	5.5%
30	5.9%
29	1.5%
28	0.7%
27	0.7%
26	0.0%
25	0.7%
<25	0.0%

Table 2.4 High, medium, and low levels (percentage) of crystallization

Group	*Percentage*
High crystallization	79,7%
Medium crystallization	12,9%
Low crystallization	2,2%

Articles and their indices can be grouped into three categories based on crystallization levels: high, medium, and low. The top three indices fall into the high crystallization category, the next three into medium crystallization, and the rest into low crystallization.[5] This grouping is presented in Table 2.4.

Considering these findings, it is possible to infer that most of the constitutional text exhibits high crystallization, with a mere 2.2% of the articles demonstrating low crystallization.

A notable limitation of the index lies in its inherent variability, as its maximum and minimum values oscillate based on the year of measurement. As the Constitution ages with each passing year, the maximum

5 Thus, articles with index 37, 36, and 35 are grouped in high crystallization (high indices), articles with index 34, 33, and 32 are grouped in medium crystallization (average indices) and articles with index 31, 30, 29, 28, or lower are grouped in low crystallization (low indices).

index value correspondingly increases. Conversely, the minimum value persistently represents the lowest observed value within the analyzed series for a given year, potentially leading to fluctuations during data collection. Consequently, comparing crystallization across disparate years becomes an arduous or even infeasible task. Therefore, in this study, the crystallization of articles less than a decade old was not quantified, as they are markedly more recent than the articles spanning 37 years. This approach was taken to preclude distortion in the overarching crystallization assessment presented in Tables 2.2 and 2.3.

To mitigate these challenges, the crystallization rate was employed. Since it operates with fixed minimum and maximum values (on a scale of 0 to 10), there is no hindrance to comparing different years. Furthermore, articles omitted from the crystallization index are included in this rate, as it factors in the specific article's age during computation. The outcomes solely derived from the rate are depicted in Table 2.5.

Owing to its absolute nature (in contrast to the relative nature of the index), the rate values show an even more crystallized composition, with no value descending below 6 (as shown in Table 2.6).

Within this metric, it is also feasible to incorporate the most recent articles that were excluded from the index. As a result, the percentage of provisions with the maximum value has increased, encompassing 50.6% of the Constitution. This phenomenon occurs because all nascent articles "commence" with the maximum crystallization rate. Given that any non-temporary legislative act is presumed to be definitive, newly introduced articles are ascribed the maximum crystallization, which decreases as they undergo amendments. The same principle applies to the constitution itself: upon promulgation, it is "born" unaltered. Only when it is subjected to its inaugural amendment does its crystallization (stability) wane.

These results reinforce the conclusion that a substantial portion of the constitutional text is crystallized, while a smaller quantity remains more fluid.

An examination of the crystallization of sections within the Constitution was also undertaken and is presented in Appendix F. In this analysis, various components of the text were categorized with crystallization indices that unveil which groupings have been most subject to changes. The organization into titles, chapters,

Table 2.5 Crystallization rate for each article in the 1988 Constitution

Art.	*Rate*	*Art.*	*Rate*	*Art.*	*Rate*	*Art.*	*Rate*	*Art.*	*Rate*	*Art.*	*Rate*	*Art.*	*Rate*	*Art.*	*Rate*
1	10.0	35	9.7	70	9.7	103-B	9.0	136	10.0	163-A	10.0	189	10.0	220	10.0
2	10.0	36	9.7	71	10.0	104	9.5	137	10.0	164	10.0	190	10.0	221	10.0
3	10.0	37	7.3	72	10.0	105	8.6	138	10.0	164-A	10.0	191	10.0	222	9.7
4	10.0	38	9.5	73	9.5	106	10.0	139	10.0	165	8.4	192	9.5	223	10.0
5	9.5	39	9.5	74	10.0	107	9.5	140	10.0	166	9.2	193	9.7	224	10.0
6	8.9	40	8.4	75	10.0	108	10.0	141	10.0	166-A	10.0	194	9.5	225	9.2
7	8.9	41	9.7	76	10.0	109	9.5	142	8.9	167	7.3	195	8.6	226	9.7
8	10.0	42	8.6	77	9.7	110	10.0	143	10.0	167-A	10.0	196	10.0	227	9.7
9	10.0	43	9.7	78	10.0	111	9.5	144	9.2	167-B	10.0	197	10.0	228	10.0
10	10.0	44	10.0	79	10.0	111-A	9.0	145	9.7	167-C	10.0	198	8.1	229	10.0
11	10.0	45	10.0	80	10.0	112	9.5	146	9.5	167-D	10.0	199	10.0	230	10.0
12	8.9	46	10.0	81	10.0	113	9.7	146-A	10.0	167-E	10.0	200	9.7	231	10.0
13	10.0	47	10.0	82	9.5	114	9.5	147	10.0	167-F	10.0	201	8.9	232	10.0
14	9.5	48	8.9	83	10.0	115	9.2	148	10.0	167-G	10.0	202	9.5	233	9.7
15	10.0	49	9.5	84	9.2	116	9.7	149	8.9	168	9.5	203	9.7	234	10.0
16	9.7	50	9.5	85	10.0	117	9.7	149-A	9.6	169	9.5	204	9.7	235	10.0
17	8.9	51	9.7	86	10.0	118	10.0	149-B	10.0	170	9.5	205	10.0	236	10.0

(*Continued*)

Table 2.5 (Continued)

Art.	*Rate*	*Art.*	*Rate*	*Art.*	*Rate*	*Art.*	*Rate*	*Art.*	*Rate*	*Art.*	*Rate*	*Art.*	*Rate*	*Art.*	*Rate*
18	9.7	52	8.9	87	10.0	119	10.0	149-C	10.0	171	9.7	206	9.2	237	10.0
19	10.0	53	9.7	88	9.7	120	10.0	150	8.9	172	10.0	207	9.7	238	10.0
20	9.5	54	10.0	89	10.0	121	10.0	151	10.0	173	9.7	208	9.2	239	9.5
21	8.1	55	9.5	90	10.0	122	10.0	152	10.0	174	10.0	209	10.0	240	10.0
22	8.9	56	10.0	91	9.7	123	9.7	153	9.2	175	10.0	210	10.0	241	9.7
23	9.5	57	9.5	92	9.5	124	10.0	154	10.0	176	9.7	211	8.9	242	10.0
24	9.7	58	10.0	93	8.6	125	9.7	155	8.1	177	8.9	212	8.9	243	9.7
25	9.7	59	10.0	94	10.0	126	9.7	156	8.6	178	9.7	212-A	6.0	244	10.0
26	10.0	60	10.0	95	9.5	127	9.5	156-A	10.0	179	10.0	213	9.7	245	10.0
27	9.5	61	9.5	96	9.2	128	9.5	156-B	10.0	180	10.0	214	9.7	246	9.7
28	9.5	62	9.7	97	10.0	129	9.7	157	10.0	181	10.0	215	9.7	247	10.0
29	8.6	63	10.0	98	9.5	130	10.0	158	9.2	182	10.0	216	9.7	248	10.0
29-A	8.8	64	9.7	99	9.7	130-A	9.0	159	8.4	183	10.0	216-A	10.0	249	10.0
30	9.7	65	10.0	100	7.8	131	10.0	159-A	10.0	184	10.0	217	10.0	250	10.0
31	10.0	66	9.5	101	9.7	132	9.7	160	9.2	185	10.0	218	9.7		
32	9.7	67	10.0	102	8.9	133	10.0	161	9.7	186	10.0	219	9.7		
33	10.0	68	10.0	103	9.5	134	9.2	162	10.0	187	10.0	219-A	10.0		
34	9.5	69	10.0	103-A	10.0	135	9.7	163	9.2	188	10.0	219-B	10.0		

Table 2.6 Percentage of Constitutional articles in different levels of crystallization rate

Rate	*Percentage*
10	50.6%
9.9 to 9	39.1%
8.9 to 8	8.9%
7.9 to 7	1.5%
6.9 to 6	0%
5.9 to 5	0%
4.9 to 4	0%
3.9 to 3	0%
2.9 to 2	0%
1.9 to 1	0%
0.9 to 0	0%

and so forth is done concentrically (nested within each other). Accordingly, any amendments that impact chapters within a title, for instance, also impact the title itself. This increases the number of amendments that a specific part of the constitution receives. What is especially intriguing in the table from Appendix F is precisely pinpointing which part of a title bears the greatest responsibility for its crystallization. This can be observed thematically (whether the instability pertains to the presidency, budget, the Union, fundamental rights, etc.).

For instance, the title pertaining to the organization of powers exhibits the lowest crystallization index. However, upon closer inspection, the chapters with the least stability are those related to the Legislative and Judicial branches. Additional scrutiny reveals that within these chapters, the sections related to the Legislative branch display high crystallization, indicating that amendments are dispersed. In contrast, within the Judicial branch, the general provisions have proven more "problematic."

Continuing with the example, the title on taxation and budget contains two chapters with low crystallization. However, the chapter on the national tax system has stabilized constituent parts, demonstrating robust crystallization rates (with revenue sharing being the least stable). This implies that these topics undergo minimal alterations. In contrast,

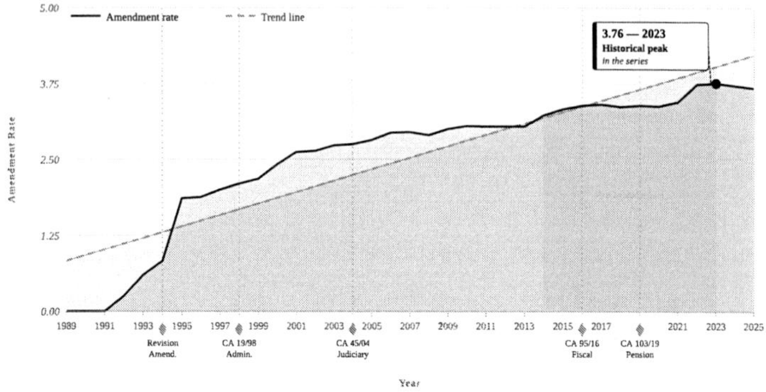

Figure 2.1 Number of amendments to the 1988 Constitution per year.

in the other chapter on public finances, the budget section is notably less crystallized, having been subject to recurrent modifications.

Despite constituting an analysis of crystallization, the results from Appendix F should not be interpreted as demonstrating a low stability of the entire constitutional text due to the instability measured in the titles, precisely because of the aspect of concentricity. The utility of this analysis lies in facilitating the identification of which themes are the subject of amendments.

On the other hand, it draws attention to the escalation in the quantity of amendments. As a result, the rate of amendment[6] to the Constitution has also increased in the last three decades, as observed in Figure 2.1. In 2023, the current Constitution reached an index of 3.76, the highest in the historical series.

In 2023, the current Constitution reached an index of 3.76, the highest in the historical series. Lutz (1994) compared amendment rates across several countries, which, although likely outdated (given that the study was conducted in 1994), can be visualized in Table 2.7.

The United Kingdom's rate remained an estimate in the study. Nevertheless, it is observed that Brazil is well above some countries and the global average, but below others that could be considered

6 Calculated by dividing the total number of amendments by the age of the Constitution.

Table 2.7 Rates of amendment for the year of 1994

Country	*Rate*
Australia	0.9
Denmark	0.17
Austria	6.3
France	0.19
Germany	2.91
Iceland	0.21
India	7.29
Japan	0
New Zealand	13.42
Portugal	6.67
Sweden	4.72
United States	0.13
United Kingdom*	7.5+
World mean	2.54

Source: LUTZ (1994, p. 369).
* *United Kingdom data remained an estimate in the study from where this information was sourced.*

consolidated democracies, such as New Zealand and Sweden.[7] Lutz also developed a methodology to identify the difficulty of amending a constitution (Lutz D., 1994, p. 368). According to this index, the Constitution can be classified with a score of 1.75 (when initiated in one of the Houses) or 1.5 (when initiated by the President of the Republic). By this measure, Brazil ranks well below the United States (5.1), Australia (4.65), Denmark (2.75), and Japan (3.1), but above New Zealand (0.5), Sweden (1.4), Portugal (0.8), and Austria (0.8) (Lutz, 1994, p. 369).

Chapter conclusions

The findings presented in this chapter demonstrate that, despite the considerable number of constitutional amendments, the Brazilian Constitution maintains substantial levels of stability in its overall structure. Quantitative analysis employing crystallization indices demonstrates that approximately 80% of articles manifest elevated crystallization, while a mere 2.2% exhibit diminished crystallization.

7 As measured in the Democracy Index of The Economist, New Zealand with an index of 9.61 (second position) and Sweden with 9.39 (fourth position) (EIU, 2023, p. 7).

This pattern of dispersion of amendments across an extensive constitutional framework, coupled with the fact that almost half of the articles remain intact since promulgation, contradicts the traditional narrative of a fragmented and ineffective Constitution. Even though certain articles—such as those pertaining to public administration, the tax system, and social security—demonstrate recurring instability, these constitute a negligible proportion of the constitutional text. A comparison with international legal systems reinforces the fact that Brazil does not deviate significantly from the pattern of amendments observed in consolidated democracies.

Given these results, it can be asserted that the ease or difficulty of amending the constitutional text will determine its adequacy or whether it fulfils the role expected of a constitution. On the contrary, the high or low degree of amendment should be aligned with the needs for effective reform in each country.[8]

Moreover, even after numerous amendments, the Constitution remains stable. In other words, the high number of amendments does not necessarily imply that the Brazilian Constitution has undergone excessive modifications affecting its consistency. While there is a small group of articles that are consistently revised and might be better suited for ordinary or complementary laws, most articles in the Constitution have been minimally revised most articles in the Constitution have been minimally revised through constitutional amendments, with nearly half of them remaining unaltered. Although the Brazilian Constitution is easily amendable, assessing its adequacy should consider the quality of the changes, a topic that will be further explored.

This suggests that the ease of amendment reflects not a constitutional deficiency but the need for dynamic adaptation to the complexities of contemporary societies. Consequently, the adequacy of the Constitution must be assessed by the substantive quality of the amendments, a topic that requires complementary qualitative analysis.

8 Lord Bryce was one of the first, if not the first, to classify constitutions into rigid and flexible, in his classic work *Studies in History and Jurisprudence*, Volume I (1901). In it, the author differentiates constitutions that are easy to change, such as that of the United Kingdom and Ancient Rome, from those that are more difficult, such as that of the USA. A part of the work that interests us is "One explanation of this apparent paradox is (though sometimes neglected) obvious enough. The stability of any constitution depends not so much on its form as on the social and economic forces that stand behind and support it)." In the same topic, see also (Edward, 1994).

References

Bryce, J. (1901). Flexible and rigid constitutions. In *Studies in history and jurisprudence* (vol. 1, pp. 124–215). Publisher: Oxford University Press. Location: New York. Fonte: https://oll-resources.s3.us-east-2.amazonaws.com/oll3/store/titles/2003/Bryce_1370.01_Bk.pdf

Edward, D. (1994). The community's constitution -- Rigid or flexible? The contemporary relevance of the constitutional thinking of James Bryce. In *Essays in Honour of Henry G. Schemers, Volume 2: Institutional Dynamics of European Integration* (pp. 57–78). Brill: Nijhoff. https://brill.com/edcollchap/book/9789004641068/B9789004641068_s009.xml

EIU. (2023). Democracy index 2022 – Frontline democracy and the battle for Ukraine. Fonte: www.eiu.com/n/campaigns/democracy-index-2022/

Han, J., Kamber, M., & Pei, J. (2012). *Data mining: Concepts and techniques.* Morgan Kaufmann. Elsevier imprint: Morgan Kaufmann Publishers: United States of America

Lutz, D. (1994). Toward a theory of constitutional amendment. *American Political Science Review,* 88(2), 355–370. Fonte: https://doi.org/10.2307/2944709

Paixão, C. (2011). Direito, politica, autoritarismo e democracia no Brasil: da Revolução de 30 à promulgação da Constituição da República de 1988. *Araucaria. Revista Iberoamericana de Filosofia, Politica y Humanidades, 13*(26), 146–169. Fonte: https://revistascientificas.us.es/index.php/araucaria/article/view/1379/1259

Stelzer, M. (2013). Constitutional change in Austria. In X. Contiades (Ed.), *Engineering constitutional change: A comparative perspective on Europe, Canada and the USA*. Routledge: London and New York. Fonte: https://dx.doi.org/10.4324/9780203094990-2

3 Qualitative analysis of amendments

Introduction

Having conducted a quantitative analysis of the amendments to address the question of their numerical impact, we now delve into the qualitative analysis, specifically focusing on the material aspect of the changes.

Examining the quality of constitutional reform undoubtedly involves a more subjective dimension, but this does not render it imprecise. Scholars dedicate themselves to investigating how the various reforms implemented in recent years have influenced the economy, civil life, public expenditure, and even the Supreme Court's interpretation of the constitution. Remarkably, even a single amendment can be the subject of divergent studies, highlighting the infeasibility of uniformly categorizing the impact of different amendments.

Methodology

The methodology employed in this work is that developed by researcher and professor Richard Albert, who classifies amendments into three categories: corrective, elaborative, and dismemberment (Albert, 2018). The choice of this methodology was driven by practical considerations (there are many amendments to be analyzed) and the belief that this classification is didactic for the purposes of this work. Albert's methodology facilitates the distinction of how a specific amendment affected the constitution. A corrective amendment can be understood as a maintenance in the text—a replacement of an element that is not functioning (or has ceased to function) with another that preserves the original intent. On the other hand, an elaborative

DOI: 10.4324/9781003679202-4

amendment can be comprehended as an upgrade, not merely the substitution of a broken part with a new one, but an improvement. This could entail granting new competencies to institutions, enhancing their capacity to fulfil their constitutional objectives, or reinforcing fundamental rights through increased safeguards, for instance.

The concept of dismemberment involves an alteration that shifts the original meaning attributed to an article or to the whole constitution, essentially changing the purpose of the constitutional document to some extent. An illustrative example comes from the reconstruction amendments in the United States, specifically amendments 13, 14, and 15 (Albert, 2018). These amendments effectively dismantled the entire constitutional framework of the original slave system, which had been established by the original framers. By undertaking this reform, the fundamental meaning of the constitution regarding the institution of slavery was significantly altered, contrary to the intentions of the authors of the US Constitution. Despite being amendments, their impact far exceeded mere corrections, as they did not advance or reinforce the slave system; instead, they led to a complete reversal of intent.

A similar classification was undertaken for the amendments that modified the Brazilian Constitution. The restrictive clause used here is not coincidental, as not all amendments altered the text of the Constitution. Some amendments solely reformed the Transitional Constitutional Provisions (ADCT), while others are entirely autonomous, akin to genuine constitutional laws[1].

It is imperative to acknowledge that the content of the ADCT is subject to the same legal hierarchy as other constitutional provisions. The ADCT functions as a legal conduit, providing a structured framework to mitigate sudden disruptions by establishing deadlines and procedural guidelines for the phased implementation of constitutional provisions, thereby regulating existing circumstances (Dantas, 1995). One of its most recent application has been to establish transitional procedures to regulate temporary electoral, administrative, and legislative processes, and to create mechanisms for the adaptation of institutions, civil servants, and public policies.

This phenomenon is indicative of the ADCT's growth. In 1988, this section of the Constitution comprised 70 articles. However, through

1 And reformed, even, by other amendments, as are the ordinary laws.

the process of constitutional amendments, it has undergone a gradual expansion, culminating in its current composition of 138 articles. This demonstrates that the ADCT functions as a flexible field within the Constitution, thus allowing constitutional legislators to address urgent and temporary changes without altering the permanent structure of the Constitution. Consequently, the articles and other provisions of the ADCT were not the subject of this research, given that their nature is eminently transitional and, to date, does not violate the fundamentals of the main constitutional text.

The qualitative analysis of the amendments was conducted in the following manner. First, a table was generated with the titles of the Constitution (Title I – Fundamental Principles, Title II, etc.). For each title, the following data were recorded: the number of articles contained therein; the number of these articles that were amended; the percentage of articles that were amended; and the number of amendments undergone by each title.. The same approach was adopted in the table for each chapter, with the titles, sections, and so on also being presented in the same manner. This allowed us to identify which titles were most amended and to analyze the amendments for each one.

The method used to classify the amendments is the one developed by Professor and researcher Richard Albert in his work *Constitutional Amendment and Dismemberment* (Albert, 2018). To recap, Albert classifies constitutional amendments into three types: corrective amendments, elaborative amendments, and dismemberment.

> Constitutional amendments come in two types: they can either be corrective or elaborative. Properly defined, a constitutional amendment is a correction made to better achieve the purpose of the existing constitution. The Twelfth Amendment to the United States Constitution, for example, is properly identified as an amendment. […] The Twelfth Amendment was designed to reduce the possibility of a tie by requiring electors to differentiate their selections for president and vice-president. It corrected a technical flaw in the original Constitution.
>
> A constitutional amendment can also be elaborative. An elaboration is a larger change than an amendment insofar as it does more than simply repair a fault or correct an error in the constitution. Like a correction, an elaboration continues the constitution-making project in line with the current design of the constitution. Instead of repairing an error in the constitution, however, an elaboration

> advances the meaning of the constitution as it is presently understood. For example, the Nineteenth Amendment is best understood as an elaborative amendment [...] The Nineteenth Amendment prohibits gender discrimination in voting, an expansion of the franchise that was not corrective in the sense of fixing a design flaw in the Constitution but was nonetheless consistent with a plain reading of equality rights as well as the existing framework of the Constitution. In this Article, I use the term amendment to refer to both corrective and elaborative amendments.
>
> (Albert, 2018, p. 3–4)

As previously explained regarding dismemberment:

> A constitutional dismemberment, in contrast, is incompatible with the existing framework of a constitution because it seeks to achieve a conflicting purpose. It seeks deliberately to disassemble one or more of a constitution's elemental parts. A constitutional dismemberment alters a fundamental right, a load-bearing structure, or a core feature of the identity of a constitution. It is a constitutional change understood by political actors and the people to be inconsistent with the constitution at the time the change is made. To use a rough shorthand, the purpose and effect of a constitutional dismemberment are the same: to unmake a constitution.
>
> (Albert, 2018, p. 4)

Using these three classifications, each of the amendments to the titles of the Constitution was analyzed. The classified amendments can be found in Appendix J, along with their respective justifications. There, the amendments are ordered as follows: amendment number with the year (heading), title (if applicable), type (according to Albert's classification), and justification for the classification used here.

The classification of the amendments was based on the changes they brought about, with reference to the text of the amendments, consultations with the parliamentary justification presented in the originating Proposed Constitutional Amendment, and the reports of the committee rapporteurs during the legislative process in both houses of Congress. The aim was to understand exactly what the proposal's intention was, why it was presented and approved, and what effects it sought to achieve.

Based on the classification of the amendments by title, a summary table was generated (also in Appendix E), ordered from the most amended title to the least, with the respective numbers (in both numerical and percentage terms) of corrective amendments, elaborative amendments, and dismemberments.

Analysis

To identify the amendments that exclusively amended the Constitution, a comprehensive study was conducted (details available in Appendix E). Based on this information, all amendments impacting the constitutional text were classified (see Appendix J). The comparison of all this data can be found in Table 3.1.

It is evident that 99 amendments have altered the Constitution, a figure lower than one might anticipate when considering the total of 138 amendments. However, what draws attention are the most frequently amended titles: "Organization of Powers" and "Organization of the State." At first glance, one might surmise that one of the most fundamental aspects of the constitution—the organization of the state and the distribution of powers—has been completely overhauled. Yet, the actual result is counterintuitive. According to Table 3.1, the preponderance of amendments in these titles are corrective in nature (72% for Organization of Powers, 84% for Organization of the State). In other words, these amendments did not fundamentally alter the character of these organizations within the Brazilian Republic. In practice, this is observable: presidentialism still prevails, the Congress remains bicameral, the Judiciary retains the same competence and independence, the Public Ministry remains unaltered, and the oversight bodies have not been abolished. In summary, the state conceived in 1988 remains essentially the same, a conclusion corroborated by the numbers.

In fact, corrective amendments constitute the visible majority across all titles, except for Title IX – General Constitutional Provisions. When examining the constitution, 72% of its amendments fall into the corrective category. Examples of such amendments include Amendment No. 4 of 1993 (which rectified the wording of the constitution to elucidate that the law altering the electoral process does not apply to the election year), Amendment No. 34 of 2001 (which emended the term "medical" to "health professionals," eliminating distortions), and Amendment No. 54 (which addressed a flaw in Revision Amendment

Table 3.1 Amendments according to the distinct parts of the Constitution

Part of the Constitution	*n° of articles*	*modified articles*		*n° of amendments*		*corrective amendments*		*elaborative amendments*		*constitutional dismemberments*	
Title IV – The Organization of the Powers	96	53	55%	36	36%	26	72%	9	25%	1	3%
Title III – The Organization of the State	27	23	85%	33	33%	27	82%	6	18%	0	0%
Title VI – Taxation and Budget	42	29	69%	32	32%	23	72%	8	25%	0	0%
Title VIII – The Social Order	44	28	64%	27	27%	20	74%	6	22%	1	4%
Title II – Fundamental Rights and Guarantees	13	7	54%	21	21%	11	52%	9	43%	1	5%
Title VII – The Economic and Financial Order	23	7	30%	10	10%	6	60%	2	20%	2	20%
Title IX – General Constitutional Provisions	18	9	50%	9	9%	4	44%	4	44%	1	11%
Title V – The Defense of the State and of the Democratic Institutions	9	2	22%	7	7%	5	71%	2	29%	0	0%
Title I – Fundamental Principles	4	0	0%	0	0%	0	0%	0	0%	0	0%
Totals	**276**	**158**	**57%**	**99**	**100%**	**71**	**72%**	**25**	**25%**	**3**	**3%**

No. 3, allowing Brazilians born abroad to be registered at consular offices).

Amendment No. 40 of 2003 serves as a quintessential example of a corrective amendment. Firstly, it rectified a patent error in the original wording of the Constitution. In the chapter on public finances, there was Section V of Article 163, which referred to "complementary law governing the oversight of financial institutions." However, this topic did not belong to that chapter. The justification for the proposed constitutional amendment, as elucidated by the rapporteur in the Chamber of Deputies, sheds light on the matter:

> In the justification, Senator José Serra, the first signatory of the proposed constitutional amendment (PEC), mentions that he was the rapporteur of the Committee on Taxation, Budget, and Finance during the National Constituent Assembly. The initial objective of Article 163 was to establish a code of public finances. Thus, the original wording of Section V was "financial oversight," clearly referring to the financial oversight of public administration. However, for some reason, during the work of the Systematization Committee, the text of Section V was modified to "oversight of financial institutions." This alteration distorted the intent of the section, as it dealt with a norm aimed at overseeing public administration, not financial institutions.
>
> (Câmara dos Deputados, 2001)

With the change, Article 163, Section V now reads "financial oversight of the direct and indirect public administration," which aligns with the original intention of the National Constituent Assembly and the theme of the chapter.

Amendment No. 40 also repealed all subsections of Article 192 of the Constitution, which pertains to the National Financial System. The original wording stipulated that a complementary law would address all the topics enumerated in Article 192's subsections, covering various areas of the financial system. However, due to political difficulties, the complementary law has not been enacted.

> The task has not been easy. In addition to the political resistance related to the validity of the real interest rate limit stipulated in § 3, the breadth of the topics listed in the article, the complexity and interaction of financial markets, and the Supreme Court's assertion

> that regulation should be carried out through a single complementary law have made it impossible to achieve the essential consensus for constructing the new financial order of the country. An eloquent testament of the difficulty in regulation is the succession of special committees established in each legislative term since 1991, which spans more than a decade, without the approval of any project or presentation of a substitute [...].
>
> The simplification of Article 192's text, through the revocation of subsections and paragraphs, and the explicit provision that regulation can be effectuated through complementary laws, aims to facilitate the task of regulation. From then on, regulation can be carried out in a fragmented manner, addressing separately the discipline of the various markets that constitute the financial system.
>
> (Câmara dos Deputados, 2001)[2]

Furthermore, in addition to the deconstitutionalization of the topic, the wording was changed to refer to "complementary laws," which rectified a flaw that hindered the regulation of the financial system. The amendment not only addressed a technical impropriety in the wording but also rectified a deficiency that complicated the political-legislative process of crafting laws that underpin the country's financial infrastructure.

Next in terms of percentages are the elaborative amendments, which advance the original constituent project. For the two most altered titles, they represent 25% and 16% of the amendments, respectively. This indicates that the intention behind these reforms was more about

2 In the original: "A tarefa não tem sido fácil. Além das resistências políticas relacionadas à vigência do limite da taxa de juros reais previsto no § 3º, a abrangência dos temas enumerados no artigo, a complexidade e interação dos mercados financeiros e a manifestação do Supremo Tribunal Federal no sentido de que a regulamentação se faça por uma única lei complementar têm inviabilizado o consenso imprescindível para a construção da nova ordem financeira do País. Prova eloqüente da dificuldade de regulamentação é a sucessão de comissões especiais instituídas a cada legislatura para este fim desde 1991, portanto há mais de dez anos, sem a aprovação de nenhum projeto ou apresentação de substitutivo [...].

A simplificação do texto do art. 192, mediante a revogação dos incisos e parágrafos, e a disposição explícita de que a regulamentação poderá ser feita em leis complementares vêm operar no sentido da facilitação da tarefa de regulamentar, porquanto a partir de então a regulamentação poderá ser realizada de forma fracionada, no conteúdo e no tempo, podendo abordar separadamente a disciplina dos diversos mercados que compõem o sistema financeiro.

reinforcing and enhancing what already existed rather than undoing it. Amendment No. 23 of 1999 serves as a good example of an elaborative type. With this amendment, the Ministry of Defense and the Commands of the Navy, Air Force, and Army were established, leading to the dissolution of the military ministries. It's not that the previous format of national defense administration necessarily couldn't continue as before, but the establishment of the new ministry and the subordination of military commands to it augmented civilian control over military activities. Furthermore, this move kept the essentially technical and highly specialized nature of military operations outside the political sphere. In conjunction with the historical context of the Constitution, written shortly after the military regime and in response to it, Amendment No. 23 advances the constituent project of control and accountability in military activities.

Moreover, examples of this type include Amendment No. 35 of 2001 (which allowed for the arrest of parliamentarians without prior permission from the legislative body to which they belong and also mandated open voting in proceedings related to the suspension of parliamentary processes, thereby reinforcing the separation of powers and democratic transparency). Additionally, Amendment No. 45 of 2004 (a comprehensive reform of the Judiciary) created bodies such as the National Council of Justice (CNJ) and the National Council of Public Prosecutors (CNMP), further enhancing transparency and efficiency in the administration of judicial services. This amendment also introduced binding precedents ("súmula vinculante"), increasing the Supreme Court's capacity to resolve conflicts. Furthermore, it placed international human rights treaties approved in two rounds by two-thirds of parliamentarians on par with amendments to the Constitution, thereby strengthening human rights protection in the country. Amendment No. 48 established the National Culture Plan, expanding the cultural system outlined in the constitution and continuing the constitutional process of valuing national culture. Lastly, Amendment No. 72 of 2013 granted equal rights to domestic workers and other classes, not only correcting a distortion but also advancing the original constituent's intention of equality among workers.

Finally, amendments resulting from dismemberment constitute a minority of the total amendments, representing a mere 3% of them. Except for Title VII (economic order) and Title IX (general constitutional provisions), all other titles have dismemberment rates below 4%, with four of these titles not even having any such amendments.

Only three amendments have been classified as dismemberments[3]. These are Amendment No. 6 of 1995 (ending the market reserve for Brazilian capital companies), Amendment No. 13 of 1996 (abolishing the Union's monopoly in the reinsurance market), and Amendment No. 114 of 2021 (changing the rules for payment of court-ordered debts to create fiscal space solely for the electoral year of 2022).

The example of Amendment No. 6 is particularly relevant as a dismemberment. Prior to the reform, the Constitution defined a Brazilian capital company as one "whose effective control is permanently under the direct or indirect ownership of individuals domiciled and resident in the country or of entities of internal public law." Effective control of the company was understood as majority ownership of its voting capital and the exercise, both in fact and in law, of decision-making power to manage its activities. Combined with Article 170, Section IX, there was constitutional protection for national capital companies at the expense of multinational companies headquartered in the country. The original constituent established a protectionist system, as provided in Article 171, paragraphs 1 and 2 of the Federal Constitution:

> Article 171, § 1 – The law may, in relation to Brazilian companies with national capital:
>
> I – grant temporary special protection and benefits to develop activities considered strategic for national defense or essential for the country's development.
>
> § 2 – In the acquisition of goods and services, the Public Administration shall provide preferential treatment, as provided by law, to Brazilian companies with national capital.

3 Here an observation about Amendment No. 95 of 2016 is warranted. It is considered a dismemberment by Richard Albert himself, who dedicates a large portion of his text explaining why. In summary, "The impact of this Public Spending Cap Amendment on the next generation's enjoyment of social rights in Brazil, combined with how directly it undermines the Constitution's founding and continuing commitment to social rights, suggests that it may be more than a simple amendment. Its purpose and effect suggest that it should instead be called a constitutional dismemberment" (Albert, 2018, pp. 40-42). Also Maués, despite not considering it as a dismemberment *per se*, understands that the aforementioned amendment would cause impacts worthy of considering it as such, since "the absolute prioritization of the reduction of the public deficit, through the containment of spending, tends to prevent the continuity of the expansion of social policies" (Maués, 2020, p. 26). Despite these arguments, we left Amendment No. 95 out of the survey because, in 2023, it was replaced by a new tax regime, implemented by complementary law, according to the order of Amendment No. 126 of 2022. Thus, if there was a dismemberment, it is in the process of reversal.

With Amendment nº 6, Article 171 was entirely revoked, and Section IX of Article 170 was altered from “favorable treatment for Brazilian small-cap companies” to “favorable treatment for small-cap companies incorporated under Brazilian laws and headquartered and managed within the country.” Consequently, there is no longer special protection for national companies, even if the majority of voting capital remains in the country. This change puts these companies on an equal footing with multinational companies based in Brazil (which are also Brazilian companies but only subsidiaries). This reversal diverges from the original intent of the constituent assembly, which envisioned a more nationalist economy in the Constitution but has since become more open and liberalized. As dismemberments are not inherently good or bad, the assessment of the Amendment nº 6 reform as positive or negative for the country will not be addressed here.

While most reforms primarily corrected the constitutional text, it is noteworthy that there was a substantial increase in the size of the Constitution. Appendices A and B make this clear (Appendix C shows the same trend in the ADCT).

As illustrated in Figure 3.1, the x-axis is indicative of the constitutional amendments in chronological order, from CA No. 1/1992 to CA No. 103/2019. The y-axis denotes the number of articles modified by each respective amendment. With regard to Appendix A, the figure adopts a horizontal perspective, offering a simplified visual rendering of the same data. As demonstrated in Figure 3.1, there were years in which the volume of change rose sharply, most visibly in the Administrative Reform (CA No. 19/1998), the Judiciary Reform (CA No. 45/2004) and the Pension Reform (CA No. 103/2019), while in others the reforms were far more modest. However, a salient feature of the graph is the predominance of darker and mid-grey tones over lighter tones. Shading is used to denote the nature of alterations: a substantial number of articles underwent purely textual modifications (mid-grey), but a considerable quantity were either expanded in scope (dark grey) or newly added (near-black), whereas comparatively few were reduced (light grey) or revoked (near-white). This pattern is confirmed at a glance by the summary strip beneath the chart, in which the darker segments clearly outweigh the lighter ones. The Constitution undergoes an increase in size rather than a decrease. This finding corroborates the work of Arantes and Couto (2019).

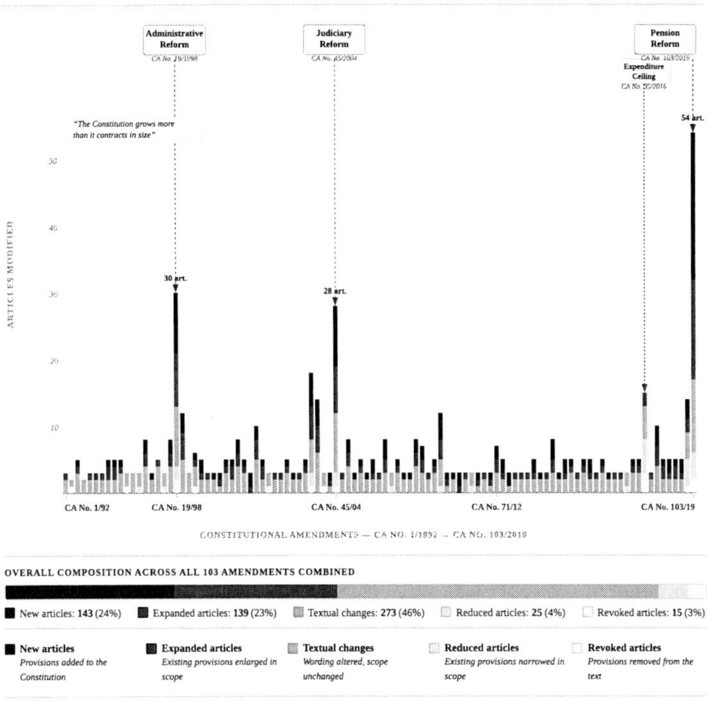

Figure 3.1 Amendments in chronological order and the number of modified articles.

Figure 3.2 provides an overview of the changes to the Constitution (the complete version is in Appendix G). The figure takes the form of a matrix: from top to bottom, the rows follow the articles in ascending order (the first row corresponds to Article 1 and the last to approximately Article 250), while from left to right the columns represent ten grouped amendment periods in chronological order, spanning CA No. 1/1992 to CA No. 103/2019.

Within the matrix, cell shading encodes the type of change, using the same greyscale as Figure 3.1: near-black for new provisions, dark grey for expanded ones, mid-grey for textual modifications, and the lightest shades for reductions and revocations; unshaded cells indicate that the article was untouched in that period. Adjacent to the matrix, a vertical strip employs a heat map to highlight the points of the text with

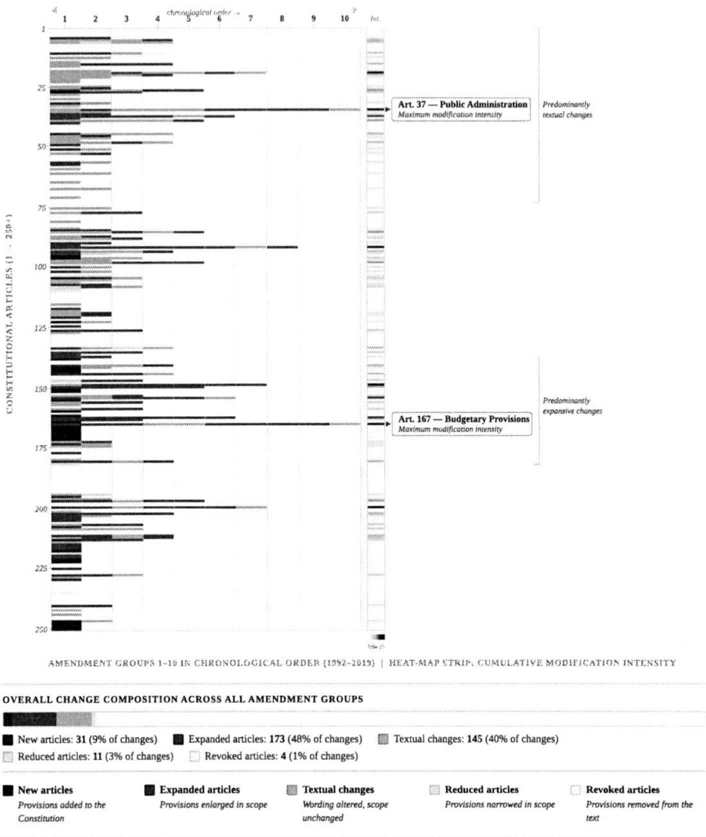

Figure 3.2 Overview of the changes in the Constitution (simplified version of Appendix G).

the most alterations: the lighter the shade, the fewer the modifications; conversely, the darker the shade (with near-black marking the maximum) the greater the cumulative number of changes.

Two points immediately stand out at the darkest end of the scale: Article 37 (Public Administration) and Article 167 (Budgetary Provisions), both flagged in the figure as recording maximum modification intensity. The two regions, however, changed in different ways.

In the upper part of the text, around Article 37, mid-grey cells predominate, meaning that this portion of the Constitution underwent mostly textual alterations. In the region of Article 167, by contrast, the darker shades prevail, suggesting that articles there were predominantly added and expanded rather than merely reworded.

Figure 3.3 reveals that the section of the Constitution dealing with the competencies of the Union, States, and the Federal District, as well as Public Administration and the responsibilities of the Congress,

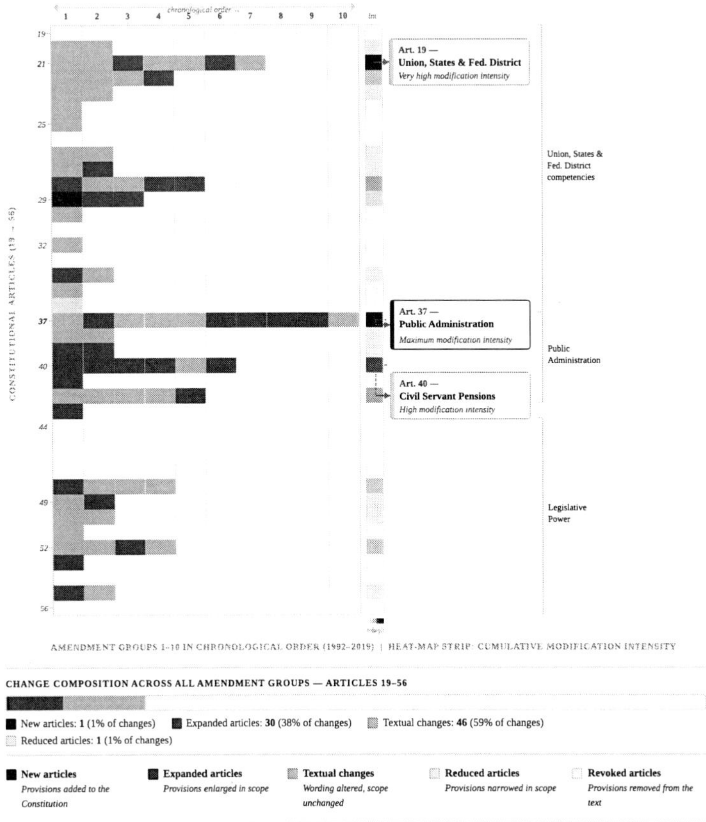

Figure 3.3 Amendments in articles 19, 37. and 56 of the Constitution.

Chamber of Deputies, and Senate, has undergone more alterations than expansions.

Conversely, Figure 3.4 (which depicts Articles 145 to 169, encompassing the limitations on the power to tax, the taxes imposed by the Union, the states, the Federal District, and the municipalities, the distribution of tax revenues, public finances, and budget) shows a predominance of modifications in the darker shades of the scale, indicating that articles in this section were chiefly added (near-black) and expanded (dark grey) rather than merely reworded. The contrast with

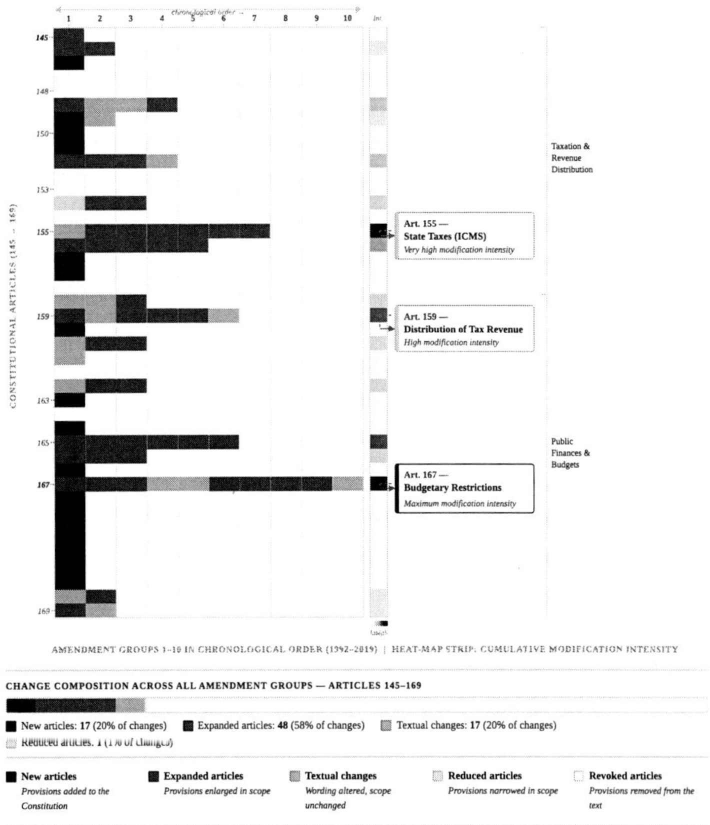

Figure 3.4 Amendments in articles 145, 159, 167, and 169 of the Constitution.

the predominantly textual profile of Figure 3.3 is reinforced by the heat-map strip, in which Article 167 (budgetary restrictions) records the maximum modification intensity, followed by Article 155 (state taxes) and Article 159 (distribution of tax revenue).

One plausible conclusion is that, in the case of Figure 3.3, the modifications may have been more in the direction of simply providing new wording for those articles, while in the case of Figure 3.4, the addition of articles, paragraphs, etc., may have occurred through the creation of new tax rules—especially related to revenue sharing—as well as supplementary rules governing the budgetary process.

It is also intriguing to observe how the Judiciary has been reformed, as shown in Figure 3.5. Two points stand out. The first is the succession of changes to the regime of court-ordered payments (*precatórios*): Article 100 records the highest cumulative modification intensity in the chapter, appearing as the darkest cell in the heat-map strip. The second is the contrast between two regions of the chapter: the Supreme Federal Tribunal area (Articles 92–103) concentrates expansive and textual changes (the darker and mid-grey shades of the matrix) whereas the Labour Court section (Articles 111–117) displays a disproportionate share of reductions and revocations, visible in the lighter shades of the scale.

Finally, an analysis of how the legislative process for amendments has changed over the last three decades is warranted. The survey can be found in Appendix I, with the Table 3.2 summarizing the data.

There is a clear predominance of amendments approved on the initiative of the Congress (88%) compared to those on the initiative of the President of the Republic (20.8%). That is, even with the ability to start the legislative process of amendment, the Executive Branch has not had a leading role in the reform of the constitution in recent years, as it had in the 1990s and early 2000s. In fact, the initiative proposals of the President of the Republic that were approved are even lower in the following decades, as can be seen in Tables 3.3, 3.4, and 3.5.

If on the one hand the number of amendments of the Executive Branch fell significantly, that of amendments of the Legislative only grew, reaching 95.6% of those approved in the last decade (Table 3.5). However, the average processing time of the President of the Republic's PCAs is much shorter than the average processing of the PCAs initiated in parliament. Within the Congress there is always a slight predominance of the Chamber of Deputies in approving amendments, but in general both Houses have a very close success rate.

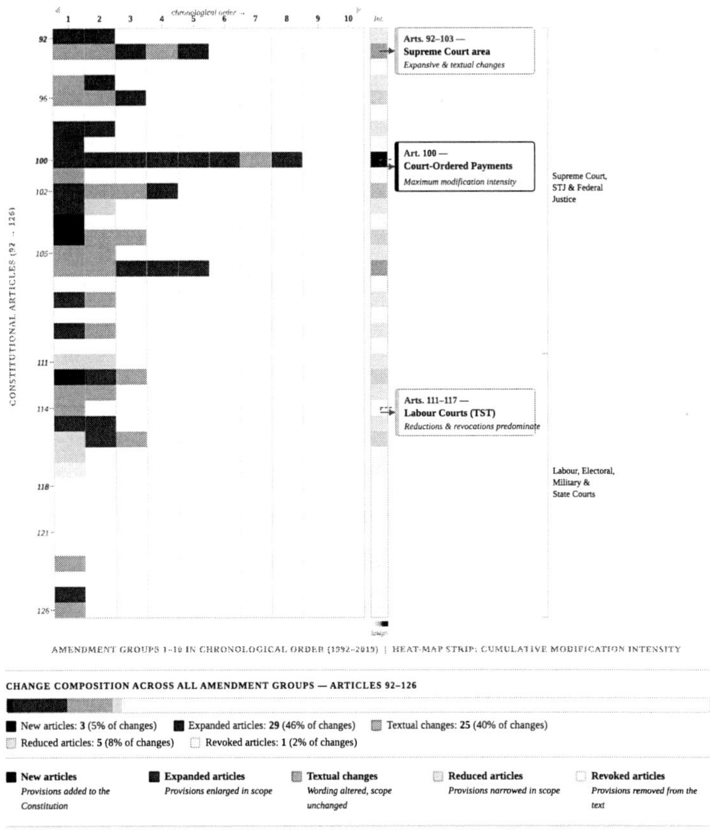

Figure 3.5 Amendments in articles 92, 100, 111, 118. and 126 of the Constitution.

This shows that the profile of the changes made in the Constitution during these years is much more defined by the composition of forces in the Congress than by projects of different governments. The performance of state governments (especially in the Senate), lobbies of economic groups and professional categories, and the various pressures that society exerts in parliament can explain why there is a clear predominance of legislative reforming action, a theme that deserves its own study.

Table 3.2 General overview

	Amendments		*Share*		*Median time of deliberation*	
Executive Power	26		20.8%		0.73	
Senate	51	110	40.8%	88.0%	4.33	4.31
Chamber of Deputies	59		47.2%		4.49	

Table 3.3 First decade

	Amendments		*Share*		*Median time of deliberation*	
Executive Power	15		42.9%		1.00	
Senate	10	20	28.6%	57.1%	3.30	3.15
Chamber of Deputies	10		28.6%		3.00	

Table 3.4 Second decade

	Amendments		*Share*		*Median time of deliberation*	
Executive Power	8		24.2%		0	
Senate	12	25	36.4%	75.8%	4.33	5.00
Chamber of Deputies	13		39.4%		5.62	

Table 3.5 Third decade

	Amendments		*Share*		*Median time of deliberation*	
Executive Power	3		4.4%		0.33	
Senate	29	65	42.6%	95.6%	4.69	4.42
Chamber of Deputies	36		52.9%		4.50	

The results in this section are consistent with another research. In the methodology adopted by Celina Souza, the amendments (up to the year 2007) were grouped into the objectives they aimed for: Redesign of the tax system—fiscal adjustment/reduction

Table 3.6 Findings of Celina Souza

Theme	*Percentage*
Fiscal policy	35%
Economic model	13%
Political-electoral system	11%
Judiciary, Legislative and legislation	11%
Executive-Legislative relations	6%
Social policy	6%
Public administration	9%
Other	9%

Source: Souza C. (2008, p. 802).

of expenditure (federal, state, municipal); Redesign of the tax system—increase of revenue (federal, state, municipal); Redesign of the economic model (breaking the monopoly of the Union and the States/opening to private capital); Redesign of the electoral and political systems; Redesign of the Judiciary (federal, state), the federal Legislative, and legal instruments; Redesign of the Executive-Legislative relationship; Transformation of rights into policies; Redesign of public administration; Design of cultural policy; Expansion of social rights; Correction of misconceptions/grey areas (Souza, 2008, pp. 800–802). From this grouping, the author arrived at the results in Table 3.6.

These data confirm what we found in our research, that most of the reforms aimed to correct issues that could be in law, not in the Constitution. The author then concludes that:

> It is concluded that the 1988 Constitution resulted from the political moment marked by the objective of making the new democratic system credible and legitimizing, given that it was drawn before the end of the transition.
>
> Not by chance, of the 62 amendments, only two changed the initial rules applicable to the political system. [...] However, and unlike what happened with the rules of the democratic system and the political system, several public policies approved by constitutional amendment have a little studied mark: they are dated, that is, they require new constitutional amendments and the return to Congress for their continuity. [...] The high rate of "amendment" of the 1988 Constitution in relation to that of other countries,

> however, does not confirm several fears from part of the literature. The first would be that constant changes in the rules of the game bring uncertainties to economic actors. In fact, changes in the economic model have opened up more opportunities for investors, both national and foreign. The second is that changes could strengthen the Executive and indefinitely extend the mandate of its leaders. [...] In addition, democratic achievements and individual, collective and social rights were not limited, and the amendments were the ones that made some social rights effective. The third would be that the Brazilian Constitution, by its extension and content (constitutionalisation of policies and rights), would prevent governability. Not only did this not happen, but the constitutional rules allowed the country to adapt to a new domestic and international agenda.
>
> (Souza, 2008, pp. 816–817)

Antônio Maués, also grouping the amendments by subject (until 2017), reached results similar to those of Souza (Table 3.7).

In this other grouping, taxation and budget matters also appear with prevalence, followed by the organization of the State and the Powers, reinforcing the reasoning that the frequent returns of the Congress to the Charter of 88 aim to correct errors or redirect fiscal and budgetary policy.

> Based on this classification, we can observe the significant domain of constitutional amendments on taxation and budget, in contrast to the relative stability of the other areas of the Constitution.

Table 3.7 Findings of Antônio Maués

Theme	*Number of amendments*
Taxing and budget	41
Organization of Powers	19
Organization of the State	17
Economic Order	8
Social Order	8
Fundamental rights	6

Source: MAUÉS (2020, p. 21).

> Even in two matters in which the number of amendments stands out—organization and defence of the State and organization of powers—several of the approved amendments had as their object themes of limited scope, whose impact on the constitutional order is very small.
>
> (Maués, 2020, p. 21)

And concludes:

> The analysis of the practice of this model showed that the distributive conflicts of Brazilian society account for most of the constitutional amendments approved. These conflicts are expressed in the constitutional order through the amendments that deal with the control of public spending and the financing of social policies [...].
>
> (Maués, 2020, p. 27)

Arantes and Couto (2006) grouped the amendments into two types (polity and policy[4]), reached very elucidative conclusions for the understanding of the amendment phenomenon in Brazil. The grouping of the two types was conducted in each of the nine titles of the Constitution, yielding the results presented in Table 3.8.

The titles with the largest number of policy-type devices (i.e. public policies) are Title IX – of the General Constitutional Provisions and Title VII – of the Economic and Financial Order. The intersection of these data with those of our research allow for two conclusions: a) the title of the General Constitutional Provisions has 50% of elaborative amendments (the highest percentage of this type) and 70% of policy-type articles, which means that the largest number of amendments occurred there, probably, because more amendments were concentrated in it aimed at deepening and advancing the existing public policies therein; and b) the opposite occurs in the title of the Economic and Financial Order, that is, although 70% of policy articles are also concentrated in it, only 11% of the amendments were elaborative, while 67% were Corrective, indicating that there was more need to correct the various public policies constitutionalized there than to

4 In the authors' definition: "**polity** corresponds to the stable parametric structure of politics, and which, it is assumed, should be as consensual as possible among the actors; [...] **policy** concerns public policies, the result of the game played according to the current rules" (Arantes & Couto, 2006, p. 47).

Table 3.8 Findings of Rogério Arantes and Cláudio Couto

Title	*Policy articles*	*Polity articles*
Fundamental principles	0%	100%
Defense of the State and of Democratic Institutions	~ 0,5%	~ 95%
Organization of Powers	~ 10%	~ 90%
Organization of the State	~ 27%	~ 73%
Fundamental Rights and Guarantees	~ 38%	~ 62%
Taxation and Budget	~ 39%	~ 61%
Social Order	~ 60%	~ 40%
Economic and Financial Order	~ 70%	~ 30%
General Constitutional Provisions	~ 70%	~ 30%

Source: Arantes & Couto (2006, p. 57).

deepen them, which may be linked to the various economic reforms made. The fact is that the Constitution concentrates many public policy articles, which means that both the government of the day and the Congress must, from time to time, revisit the Charter:

> The Brazilian political and governmental agenda remains a constituent agenda, not because successive presidents wanted to mutilate the fundamental principles or for another exogenous reason, but because the Charter itself forced them to amend the Constitution to implement public policies.
>
> (Arantes & Couto, 2006, p. 58)

Noteworthy is the Supreme Court's performance in the amendment process. Oliveira and Arguelhes (2021) conducted a survey of ADIs (Direct Actions of Unconstitutionality) filed and judgments by the Supreme Court to understand how the court interferes with constitutional changes initiated by the Congress. They analyzed 105 amendments, of which 35 were subject to ADI, with the highest number of ADIs per amendment being for Amendment No. 41 of 2003 (pension reform, with 25 ADIs), No. 45 of 2004 (judiciary reform, with 16 ADIs), and No. 20 of 1998 (pension reform, with 13 ADIs). Together, they account for 44% of the actions (Oliveira & Arguelhes, 2021, p. 4). By classifying the types of provisions questioned using Arantes and Couto's (2006) methodology, they found that 78% of the actions questioned only policy aspects, while 17% questioned only polity aspects, and 5% questioned both aspects (Oliveira & Arguelhes, 2021, p. 7). Regarding the outcome of these actions, the Supreme Court did not hear or ruled as moot 30% of the requests and dismissed another 11% on the merits. The court ruled as granted, in whole or in part, 9% of the requests, and granted injunctions in another 11%, meaning the Court interfered in 42.8% of the 35 amendments brought to ADIs. The main authors of the actions were magistrates' associations and then defeated political parties in the legislative process (Oliveira & Arguelhes, 2021, pp. 8–9). The authors concluded that:

> The descriptive data presented here show that, in Brazil, the judicial challenging of constitutional amendments is a frequent phenomenon that is as much a part of the national political process as the adoption of the amendments themselves. […] In particular, magistrates' associations have established themselves as the primary 'clients' of the STF's abstract logic of judicial review when questioning Constitutional Amendments, systematically seeking to defend their corporate interests. […] The threat of judicial intervention in the production of amendments has materialized frequently enough to be considered an integral part of Brazilian constitutional politics.
>
> (Oliveira & Arguelhes, 2021, pp. 15–16)

The high number of public policies inscribed in the constitutional text ends up inviting a greater participation of the Judiciary in the amendment process, considering them sometimes unconstitutional[5].

With this, we reach the third and final conclusion of this study: the Constitution has not been significantly altered relative to the 1988 text, given that 72% of the reforms carried out were corrective in nature and 25% were elaborative—changes that maintain the original orientation of the framers. Nevertheless, there is a visible increase in the constitutional text across its entire length. This expansion, linked to the prevalence of legislative action in the reforms of the last two decades, indicates that partisan political maneuvering is responsible for this growth. Furthermore, the high volume of provisions

5 About that, see Tulis (1988), Roznai (2013), and Novelli (1995). On the debate between the Legislative and the Judiciary, see Hachem & Pethechust (2021).

regarding public policies makes the use of the derivative constituent process recurringly necessary, while rendering the involvement of the Judiciary relatively expected.

Chapter conclusions

A thorough qualitative analysis of the Brazilian constitutional amendments reveals that, despite the considerable number of reforms that have been promoted since 1988, most of them (72%) are corrective in nature, remaining faithful to the original constitutional architecture. The extensive amendments (25%) served to elaborate and reinforce existing provisions, while constitutional dismantling represented a mere 3% of the total.

There has been a visible and continuous expansion of the constitutional text, a phenomenon linked to the predominance of legislative action in the reforms of the last two decades and the growth of provisions on constitutionalized public policies. This combination of factors has resulted in a reform process with reduced presidential involvement, and which now more accurately reflects the political and corporate pressures exerted on Congress. Consequently, the recurrent use of the derivative constituent process has become necessary for the continuous implementation of public policies, while the involvement of the Judiciary in the validation of constitutional amendments has become an integral part of Brazilian constitutional policy.

Although the current Constitution retains its structural elements, it is undergoing a permanent process of constitutionalization that reflects the distributive dynamics of Brazilian society.

References

Albert, R. (2018). Constitutional amendment and dismemberment. *Yale Journal of International Law,* 43(1), 1–84. Retrieved from https://openyls.law.yale.edu/bitstream/handle/20.500.13051/6721/RichardAlbertConstitution.pdf?sequence=2

Arantes, R., & Couto, C. (2006). Constituição, Governo e Democracia no Brasil. *Revista Brasileira de Ciências Sociais,* 21(61), 41–62. Fonte: https://doi.org/10.1590/S0102-69092006000200003

Arantes, R., & Couto, C. (2019). 1988–2018: Trinta anos de constitucionalização permanente. In N. Filho & A. Souza (Eds.), *A Carta: para entender a Constituição brasileira.* Todavia: São Paulo, Brazil.

Câmara dos Deputados. (2001). *Comissão Especial destinada a proferir parecer à proposta de emenda à constituição nº 53-a/1999, que altera o inciso v do art. 163 e o art. 192 da constituição federal, e o caput do art. 52 do ato das disposições constitucionais transitórias.* Brasilia: BRASIL. Câmara dos Deputados. Fonte: www.camara.leg.br/proposicoesWeb/prop_mostrarintegra?codteor=9310

Dantas, I. (1995). Das disposições constitucionais transitórias: uma redução teórica. *Revista de Direito Administrativo*, 199, 79–87.

Hachem, D., & Pethechust, E. (2021). A superação das decisões do STF pelo Congresso Nacional via emendas constitucionais: diálogo forçado ou monólogos sobrepostos? *Revista de Investigações Constitucionais,* 8, 209–236.

Maués, A. (2020). 30 Anos De Constituição, 30 Anos De Reforma Constitucional. *Revista Direito GV,* 16(1), 72–101. Fonte: https://doi.org/10.1590/2317-6172201941

Novelli, F. (1995). Norma Constitucional Inconstitucional? A propósito do art. 2º, § 2º, da Emenda Constitucional nº 3/93. *Revista de Direito Administrativo,* 199, 21–57.

Oliveira, F., & Arguelhes, D. (2021). O Supremo Tribunal Federal e a Mudança Constitucional. *Revista Brasileira de Ciências Sociais,* 36(105), 1–20. Fonte: https://doi.org/10.1590/3610506/2020

Roznai, Y. (2013). Unconstitutional constitutional amendments---The migration and success of a constitutional idea. *American Journal of Comparative Law,* 61(3), 657–720.

Souza, C. (2008). Regras E Contexto: As Reformas Da Constituição De 1988. *Dados,* 51(4), 791–823. Fonte: https://doi.org/10.1590/s0011-52582008000400001

Tulis, J. (1988). The demon at the center. *The University of Chicago Law Review,* 55(2), 548–554.

Conclusion

The analytical journey undertaken throughout this work, which covers the historical, quantitative, and qualitative dimensions of Brazilian constitutional amendments, reveals a paradoxical institutional phenomenon that challenges established narratives about the fragmentation of the 1988 Brazilian Constitution. It is a commonly held view that the number of amendments in a constitution is indicative of the degree of constitutional instability. However, the data collected and analyzed in this study demonstrate that the Constitution, despite having undergone numerous reforms, has maintained a remarkably preserved essential structure.

The cathedral metaphor, introduced at the beginning of the book, is particularly apt for summarising the conclusions presented. The Brazilian Constitution, much like the great European cathedrals that were constructed over centuries and subsequently enlarged, renovated, and improved by successive generations, has undergone a similar development. Its foundations have remained intact, while layers of modifications have been added, which are not always visible at first glance, but whose cumulative impact has produced a more robust, albeit more complex, institutional edifice than it was initially. The assumption of constitutional fragility resulting from the various amendments does not withstand the methodological scrutiny undertaken here.

Is the Brazilian Constitution of 1988 the same?

In 1889, when Brazil transitioned from a monarchy to a republic, the national flag underwent modifications in its design. The yellow diamond, which was inscribed in a green rectangle, was placed on a

DOI: 10.4324/9781003679202-5

green field (the tips of the diamond no longer touch the edges of the flag), and the Imperial Arms were replaced by the republican celestial sphere. These were subtle changes that preserved the identity (the essence, so to speak) of the national pavilion, making clear the shift in regime, without altering the nation's core identity.

However, the same did not happen to the Constitution. The Imperial Constitution from 1824 was abolished, and in its place, a new Constitution was promulgated in 1891, heavily inspired by its American counterpart. This shift marked a formal break in political and legal frameworks. Yet, in practice, the constitutional changes did not bring about a radical transformation in the country's political structure. The same political class, economic elite, and power brokers remained in control. In essence, while the Constitution changed on paper, the real dynamics of power stayed largely the same.

The Imperial Constitution could have been amended so that it could be transformed into a Republican Law, with few modifications to fit the emerging regime, avoiding a complete break from the monarchical past. This might have prevented some of the crises that plagued the First Republic. However, the Constitution did not follow the example of the flag. It was perhaps at this moment that the recurring practice—almost a norm—began: replacing an unwanted regime with a new and supposedly better one through constitutional overhaul. Of course, Brazil was not unique in this approach. As seen in the cases of Germany and France, both nations also went through multiple national charters and constitutions.

But specifically in the Brazilian case, the practice has always been trying to solve political problems through new constitutions. Here, a counterfactual exercise: it is possible to imagine that the Constituent Assembly of 1890 could have simply amended the old constitution—as has already been suggested. But even if they insisted on a new Constitution for the country at the end of the 19th century, was another one truly necessary in 1934? There was no significant constitutional break between these two regimes, as we were still a republic, still presidentialist, still federalist. But one might argue that the 1934 regime inaugurated a national practice of constitutional concern with social matters, the family, and the economic order. Beyond that, the text remained quite similar.

What, then, was the necessity to promulgate a new charter in 1946? The original constituent power, plenipotentiary as it is, could have easily used the classic legislative phenomenon of repristinating—authorized when done explicitly—to reinstate the 1934 Constitution, arguing, for instance, that it had been improperly revoked by the Vargas government.

The case of the 1967 Constitution is even more striking. The military dictatorship arrogated to itself the power to amend the constitution unilaterally and at its own discretion through institutional acts. What was the need for a Fundamental Law to replace the 1946 one when they could remodel it as they wished? They certainly did this in 1969, even with the 1967 Constitution.

The historical research conducted in Chapter 1 has revealed that the current Brazilian Constitution is not an entirely original act, but rather the result of a "constitutional transfer" that incorporates elements from virtually all previous Brazilian constitutions. The "Historical Constitution"—this institutional fabric that runs through the various Brazilian constitutional charters since 1824—demonstrates that the deliberations of the 1987–1988 constituents did not occur in a vacuum, but within a complex and multifaceted institutional tradition. The index of proximity of constitutional genealogies to the 1988 text reaches high values, indicating not a radical break, but an incremental evolution of the Brazilian constitutional order.

This exercise shows that Brazil has always preferred to inaugurate a new constitution when it wanted to change the dynamics and exercise of power. It is undeniable that every new Constitution carries symbolic meaning, bringing with it the celebration of a new era, a new attempt to move the country forward. However, as this work demonstrated, rather than creating entirely new constitutions, Brazil has continuously built upon the "same" constitution—through additions and reforms—what we might call its *historical constitution*. Much like the centuries-old European cathedrals, which began modestly and were expanded, renovated, and refined over generations—work measured not in years but in decades or even centuries—our constitutionalism has followed a similar path, layering each new constitution on the foundations of the past. It is our "Cathedral Constitution."

The Cathedral Constitution

Not only can we view Brazil's historical constitution as a "Cathedral," but the current Constitution also fits this metaphor. As we have seen, the numerous amendments show that the country's constituent process is almost continuous. In keeping with constitutional tradition, legislators who amend the 1988 Constitution rarely break with the past; instead, they build upon what already exists. This work has demonstrated that most amendments have been corrective in nature, some have expanded on the original framework, and only a few have significantly altered the direction set in 1988.

The quantitative analysis in Chapter 2 served to consolidate this understanding. The methodological application of the crystallization index and crystallization rate revealed that approximately 80% of the articles of the Constitution demonstrate elevated levels of crystallization. It is evident that the majority of articles have not undergone frequent modifications, remaining stable throughout the three decades of the Constitution's existence. A particularly noteworthy finding is that approximately 43% of the constitutional articles have remained unamended since 1988.

As is apparent from the analysis, while certain constitutional provisions—notably those pertaining to public administration, the tax system, and social security—evince recurring instability, these constitute a negligible proportion of the constitutional text, representing merely 3.6% of the total articles. The pattern of dispersion of amendments across an extensive constitutional framework refutes the traditional narrative of a fragmented and ineffective Constitution. International comparison has also yielded instructive results. A comparison of Brazil's amendment rate with that of other consolidated democracies reveals that Brazil does not deviate significantly from the pattern of constitutional reforms observed in established democratic regimes.

The "cathedrality" of the Constitution becomes very evident this way. It was, and continues to be, built by many generations of lawmakers. And just like Cathedrals, the Constitution keeps growing, gaining additions and sections full of details. Despite these reforms, it has not lost its original essence and function, still maintaining the same foundations and structures that sustain the entire national legal order.

The qualitative analysis conducted in Chapter 3 constituted the final, and arguably most significant, element of this investigation. The methodology developed by Richard Albert, which categorizes amendments as corrective, elaborative, and dismemberment, demonstrated that 72% of all Brazilian constitutional amendments were of a corrective nature. In essence, the majority of reforms aimed to rectify, elucidate, or enhance the constitutional text, thereby safeguarding the original intent of the constituents. A mere 25% of the proposed amendments were considered to be elaborative, seeking to advance the original constitutional project. A further 3% were classified as dismemberment—that is to say, those amendments that reversed fundamental elements of the Constitution as conceived in 1988.

In the qualitative dimension, a particularly significant phenomenon was identified: the textual expansionism of the Constitution. While the majority of amendments are of a corrective nature, the constitutional text has expanded significantly. This is indicative of the constitutionalization of public policies and the predominance of legislative action in the reforms of the last two decades. This growth does not necessarily indicate a weakness in the Constitution, but rather the incorporation of matters that could have remained within the domain of infra-constitutional legislation. Indeed, the research suggests that the removal of certain topics from the constitutional sphere would reduce the need for frequent amendments, thereby improving normative stability.

Despite its 138 amendments, the Brazilian Constitution continues to fulfil the historical role assigned to Fundamental Laws, as outlined in this work. Constitutions are typically drafted to define civil rights, structure government, and establish the political relationships within a country. Essentially, a people occupying a given territory decide to set forth the rights and duties that will govern their political community, while instituting a government to enforce them. Hobbes referred to this as the "sleeping sovereign," with the government acting on its mandate. In modern terms, we might say that the government operates on autopilot until sectors of society intervene to change its course.

The Constitution has undergone only corrective changes in its essence and remains fundamentally the same. This work does not aim to assess whether the amendments since its promulgation are good or bad—that is a question for further research and broader societal debate. Instead, our goal was to show that, despite these amendments, the core of the Brazilian Constitution remains intact. Rather than repeating the historical pattern of drafting new constitutions, there is no need for a new one. Instead, we should harness the existing reformist momentum to "deconstitutionalize" certain issues and address them through infraconstitutional legislation.

The findings of the present study carry considerable implications for Brazilian constitutional policy. Firstly, the assertion that the 1988 Constitution is a "failed Constitution" that must be entirely rewritten is refuted. The data suggest that, despite its imperfections and the need for improvements, the Constitution has provided a reasonably stable institutional framework that has been adaptable to the social, political and economic changes of the last 38 years.

Another salient aspect of the work was the critical distinction between the quantity and quality of amendments. The multiplication of constitutional reforms, in itself, does not signify political dysfunction or institutional inadequacy. Conversely, within the context of social dynamics and political pressures, it can be considered a legitimate and necessary institutional response. The ease or difficulty with which a constitution can be amended is not indicative of its adequacy or its ability to fulfil its role as fundamental law. Conversely, the intensity of constitutional reforms must be aligned with the needs for effective reform in each country.

A third element that has been brought to light by the research points to the importance of improving the design of the Brazilian constitution. The identification of "problem areas," i.e. articles that undergo recurring amendments, suggests that these matters could be more appropriately addressed in ordinary or complementary legislation. The argument was substantiated that such an adjustment would not weaken the Constitution; on the contrary, it might even strengthen it. This is because it would reduce unnecessary pressure on the derivative constitutional process and allow for greater normative stability.

The experience with several federal laws that have governed the country for a long time, demonstrate that it is perfectly possible to leave the regulation of society to ordinary and complementary laws, especially when it comes to public policies, which, as we have seen, make up a significant portion of the Constitution's articles. In many democratic countries, it is common practice to address policy issues through ordinary legislation, allowing the prevailing political agenda, regardless of ideology, to be implemented more effectively. Unlike cathedrals, our Cathedral Constitution can be reduced.

Finally, the Constitution is viewed as a "cathedral," a perspective which offers a more comprehensive perspective on contemporary Brazilian constitutionalism and, perhaps, on constitutionalism practiced in other democracies. Just as the construction of great cathedrals was not completed in a single generation, but rather through successive contributions from master builders, craftsmen, and reformers from different centuries, the Brazilian Constitution is also the result of a long-term constitutional project. Each amendment, reform, or regulatory adjustment is a deliberate attempt to address deficiencies in the present system while remaining faithful to its foundational principles. As is evidenced by the numerous instances of works that have been unsuccessful or have necessitated complete reconstruction, a similar phenomenon can be observed in the context of cathedrals. In the context of constitutional reform, there is always a possibility of failure, yet it is evident that there is no inherent structural damage.

The Brazilian Constitution, far from being a fragile structure on the verge of collapse, is in fact a flexible yet robust framework. It is a living institution that adapts and evolves, absorbs social pressures and political demands, and incorporates lessons learned from its own application. The edifice, in essence, is a cathedral under perpetual reconstruction; a structure whose inherent stability is evidenced precisely by its capacity to accommodate change without compromising its fundamental identity.

The future of Brazilian constitutionalism will be contingent not on radical replacement of the Constitution with a new one, but rather on the continuity of a more reflective, judicious constitutional reform process focused on the substantive quality of the changes. Should this course of action be pursued, the "constitutional cathedral" will not only withstand the pressures of the present, but will remain, as is its proper function, the foundation upon which political institutions are established.

Index

For Product Safety Concerns and Information please contact our EU representative GPSR@taylorandfrancis.com Taylor & Francis Verlag GmbH, Kaufingerstraße 24, 80331 München, Germany